Ghost Night: Wednesday

Ghost Night: Wednesday

✦

(Counseling the Dead)

Reverend Jeri Wahinehookai, PhD

iUniverse, Inc.
New York Lincoln Shanghai

Ghost Night: Wednesday
(Counseling the Dead)

iUniverse, Inc.

For information address:
iUniverse, Inc.
2021 Pine Lake Road, Suite 100
Lincoln, NE 68512
www.iuniverse.com

ISBN: 0-595-31198-9

Printed in the United States of America

THIS BOOK IS DEDICATED TO...

*My Mother
Lorraine Sanderson Briggs
(1918–2003)
For Giving Me Life
And Teaching Me Love*

and

*All Other Divine Beings
Who Support and Assist Me*

Contents

Acknowledgements

Special Thanks To:

Roy Kiyoshi Goya, Susan Lee Brown

all of our clients who give us their trust and honor our work,
all souls we have met in the ethers

The Mothership Maui Tribe

Karen Saura for her editing expertise

Suzanne Joyce for her time and skills

Captain Reuben Lono Wahinehookai, My Husband
who supports my path

Lori De Hoog
my sister, my friend

Joey and Trish Hines
my son and daughter-in-law, my beloved fans

Sophia Maria Wahinehookai
my daughter, my teacher

Introduction

A research group was formed in 1986 through the desire of several individuals to explore metaphysics as it applies to the body, mind and spirit. We wanted to develop tools for the purpose of healing and balancing our inner and outer selves and to enhance our professional practices.

I was asked to create a weekly study group in my home, on the island of Maui, Hawaii. I agreed, with one stipulation, which was that we focus on the Huna psycho/spiritual philosophy as our base. Some refer to this philosophy as a religion but it is far more than that. Huna embodies a code of ethics to live by, a way of "being" in every aspect of one's daily life, not just an affiliation with a church attended once a week or on religious occasions. Huna embodies the Universal Principles, or Laws of Nature, as taught through the study of metaphysics.

We had all been involved in some aspect of metaphysical knowledge or practices, which we wanted to exchange and expand upon. These and other skills and knowledge brought into the group by members include: Psychic Sensitivity, Hawaiian Body Massage (lomi lomi), Nursing; Hypnotherapy, Parapsychology, Sexual Assault/Abuse and Family Abuse Counseling, Youth and Family Social Services, Montessori Teaching, Native American Philosophy and Ceremony, Gemstone Therapy, Color and Toning Therapy, Divination, Astrology and Numerology (occult sciences). The common thread for us was service in the counseling/healing professions in a spiritual atmosphere.

The focus was to enhance what each person brought into the research to improve our skills and expand our personal reality through understanding the non-physical aspects of the body, mind and spirit. To this day, our greatest tools have been our sense of humor and our willingness to commit to ourselves, our research and each other in friendship; for the purpose of our psycho/spiritual growth, personally and professionally.

The group became a "tribe", a merging of men and women of various ages and cultural, racial and religious backgrounds, blending Euro-American, Hawaiian, Japanese, Filipino, Hispanic, Native-American Indian and others. Our collective background of religious/spiritual teachings includes: Catholic, Protestant, Buddhist, Christian Science, Mormon, Muslim, Huna, and various nature based philosophies.

We began to see the effects of our work in ourselves and in others, on a daily basis, in all areas of our lives. This is where the work really begins and continues for anyone who makes a commitment to assist another or teach in the healing arts—healing the self! This is the first order of business for anyone who professes a desire to be of professional service to others in any capacity.

Eventually, we were asked to do various services for others such as clearing/blessing of people, places and things. I began to give workshops sharing the various tools and processes we used. The Rainbow Journey is a meditative inner process reconnecting people with their inner child aspect. This is the very basic first step to assist in accessing all other procedures listed in the Toolbox chapter. The Spirit-release or "clearing" process is the main focus of this book, which includes the Ho'oponopono ceremony. We have presented these workshops throughout Hawaii and have given radio interviews. Some of us volunteer our skills and tools to a youth group of emotionally troubled children, here on Maui.

We network our information through writings, cassette tapes, alternative/complimentary healing practices and various psychic/spiritual services. In our second year we were encouraged to publish a quarterly newsletter to share our tools and information, which we did for two years. I then wrote a workbook, *Mothership Maui: The Journey Beyond*, with the tools and processes for clients and others who wanted the information. This was done with great assistance from Suzanne Joyce, of the group (that workbook is included in this book).

The studies and practical experiences within the experimental atmosphere of the group and our clientele have greatly accelerated our professional work. We have been able to incorporate the tools, creating holistic application in our practices. The main focus of this book is about the deceased and their influence on the embodied, including transcripts of actual Spirit Release sessions with clients. The book speaks to all those loved ones or practitioners involved with them. I also describe the tools and philosophy we work from in doing this work, as I consider them to be the vital ingredients for our success.

The call for our Spirit release services began to increase early on, and we decided to designate one night a week for this work. That night was Wednesday. Eventually, we couldn't do all the weekly requests in one night. Our caseload rose to between three and six sessions per week, but Wednesday is still our main ghost night!

The whole group has participated at one time or another in expansive Spirit Release of businesses and/or land. Roy Goya, Suzanne Joyce and myself did the clearings for individuals for several years. Susan Brown has been my work partner for the past couple of years. All group members are sensitives (psychics) of one "type" or another or a combination. All psychics have a dominant channel (frequency) they receive through, most often. Roy is a very strong clairvoyant (to see) and clairsentient (whole body knowing). Susan is predominantly a clairempathic (to feel) and clairvoyant. Suzanne Joyce is clairempathic and clairsentient. I am predominantly clairsentient and clairaudient (to hear). We all receive on any of those frequencies at different times, depending on the nature of a situation.

The Research

All of our tools, processes and the Huna philosophy fall under the category of metaphysics. The word metaphysics means "beyond the physical." Dictionaries have several other definitions, including "the study of the real nature of things" and "highly abstract, hard to understand." It doesn't need to be hard to understand if we have an open mind and are willing to integrate scientific and spiritual realities. Only man, in his fear, ignorance or greed has created the separation of the two realms. They are not exclusive—in nature all is relative.

One category of metaphysics is the occult sciences (Astrology, Numerology, Divination, etc.) The word occult, itself is greatly misunderstood. Some dictionary meanings are: concealed, secret, beyond the bounds of ordinary knowledge, mysterious, mystic, outside the laws of the natural world, revealed only to the initiated (in early science), not apparent on mere inspection—but discoverable by experimentation. Synonym: metaphysical.

As you can see, some definitions imply that the natural world is limited to the physical, which is a misunderstanding of natural laws. There was quite a lot negative stigma put upon the subject of metaphysics, which was created intentionally, by those in authority, who wanted control over the masses. They did not want the people to discover their own innate abilities, to direct their own lives through an understanding of the nature of Spirit in all things—animate and inanimate. In truth, metaphysics clarifies the Natural Laws and the Spiritual nature of our reality.

Many people are fearful of these subjects. Usually, they are fearful of the unknown or the "bad press" given to other-worldly topics. There is extensive misinformation and disinformation on metaphysical subjects and many misguided practitioners. This has contributed to experiences, which are perceived as negative. Most can be easily explained. Fear can be created by abuse of power but more often it is caused by a person's limited perceptions. You might ask, "Why bother? Why not leave my fears alone?" Because unprocessed fear creates limitation and blockage to emotional balance and physical health.

Fear is a dark cloud over the lens of the mind, which often creates negative distortion of an otherwise harmless thing that can be made clear through understanding.

The nature of our work is the exploration of the metaphysical reality of our world and how it affects our lives, specifically the non-physical reality of the self in relation to the well-being of the body, mind and spirit.

I wish to share our research with you and encourage your further exploration of these subjects. Knowledge of the metaphysical reality of our selves and our world is of vital importance to our survival, now and in the future.

The Dying (A Memorial)

Kimo is very weak this morning—is today the day? A question we have all had each day for the last month, ever since the doctor told us that his health condition was terminal.

Kimo has been a beloved friend of mine for the last twenty years. He is being cared for in a cottage behind my house. Our friend, Suzanne, lives there and has agreed that we bring Kimo here to die. Assisting us with his full-time care is another mutual friend, Peggy. Kimo's home was in his Ford van for the last several years, until the exploratory surgery for a chronic health condition. He needs care and bed rest now.

Suzanne is arranging the sheets and pillows as Kimo sits on a stool. He is suddenly much weaker than before and needs help. I hold him up and massage his shoulders, which are aching now. He knows…He remarks, *"It will be soon now."*

For weeks, Suzanne and I have sat with him, talking of death and what might be on the "other side" for him. We have shared our belief that we are immortal, but he is still very fearful. Kimo is only fifty-seven years old, it seems too soon…but he has said, "I have had a full life and I'm ready."

A part of him wants out of that body which was crippled by polio as a young child. He endured great pain and discomfort through many surgeries and extended hospital time during his childhood. Those surgeries were part of an experimental program of that time. Ultimately, one leg was most affected and it was atrophied causing a severe limp.

Polio has never stopped him from being a totally professional musician all his life. Yes, he had buried anger, which is what liver cancer is about at an emotional level. I mentioned to him, one time, that polio was a condition that was connected to an emotional pattern of jealousy. I asked him, "Are you jealous?" He said, in a firm tone, *"Yeah!"* I said, "Really, of who or what?" He said, *"Everything and everyone!"* I was rather surprised because I had not been aware of the depth of those feelings in him.

He was a real-life Hawaiian "beach-boy" in his youth when all the big ships came to Honolulu. The "boys" would dive for coins tossed overboard by the passengers. They would sing and play music to the visitors on the beaches. He was physically able to do all the things any "local boy" could do: diving, throwing net (fishing), dancing, driving and more. He loves food, as many Hawaiians do, and he is a great cook.

Kimo has a great love for the animal kingdom, including the ones he doesn't eat. His nickname for my dog, Moki, is "huli dog", which is loosely translated as barbeque dog. Of course, he was just kidding, I think. However, he has eaten his share of dog. Kimo has also saved and cared for many critters and always protests to those who are not kind to any animal. Kimo loves and cares for children with the same guardianship.

A favorite activity and therapy for Kimo is gardening. He can do magic with any plant he touches. He treats them as the living beings they truly are. On several occasions he has turned a desolate piece of land into a beautiful garden or a cropland.

Kimo was blessed with an incredible voice, with a wide octave range and a deep resonance. His voice penetrated your body & his delivery of the song pulled you into the story and the melody of it. His articulation was very clear. He sang a great variety of songs of various cultures. I feel he sang very healing tones for many who came to listen.

This local boy from Oahu has traveled all over the mainland and the South Pacific and lived in San Diego, California for a few years. He is a wonderful artist and wood carver. He designed costumes and headdresses for the dancers in the Polynesian musical shows, where he also played drums, guitar and sang. He played with Martin Denny for a time and later had his own trio. Kimo is a consummate Hawaiian musician/entertainer, with a wonderful sense of humor and an intense passion for his culture.

Kimo is ready to go back to bed, but he is so weak he cannot stand. Suzanne and I lift him onto the bed, in a slightly reclining position. His whole body aches from his toxic condition (gall bladder/liver cancer). As he lay back onto the pillows he says, *"OK, what do we do now?"* I respond, "we just relax and breathe." I begin to massage his feet. Suzanne sits on the bed with him, holding and stroking his hand.

Last night, Kimo was able to watch a special boxing match. Boxing is a favorite sport and he was dissapointed when he thought he had missed it. Our friends, Acy and Tony had taped it for him, which gave him great delight. He has eaten all his favorite foods during the past month, given most of his belongings to those he wanted to have them and said "aloha" to all those he wanted to contact. He has forgiven most of the people who have ever "pissed him off," and thanked others for their part in his life.

He asked to be cremated and wants his ashes put under the Japanese orchid tree (a gift from him), outside in my yard. I said I would do that. Two of his family members want some of the ashes, so he has told them they could have them, with a stipulation. He said, *"Throw me any place you like, but not in the ocean."* They agreed, as everyone laughed.

Early on, Suzanne called Hospice to assist Kimo and all of us through the waiting time. According to the doctors it would be three to six months. Such a difficult time for all concerned, which has been made easier by the two Hospice caretakers. One is a nurse, Evelynn, and the other is Prakash, a counselor. Kimo likes both of them very much and they seem to really enjoy his humor and his stories

Kimo has been in a sort of "cram-course" on dying and what may lie beyond. He does not want to linger in this condition and has obviously accelerated his departure time. He has already planned to "give me a sign" after he is on the other side. I asked him what kind of sign? We could prearrange it. He said, *"No, you'll know when it happens."* I told him that was fine, but we would also be talking to him on the other side, to check in on him. He just grinned and said, *"Nahh."*

He is beginning to relax more now and his breathing is less strained…the room is silent, except for our breath…I can't even hear the birds outside. There is a very specific rhythm to his breathing, with a subtle drumming as accompaniment…I feel drawn in to the flow…it is strangely soothing. We find ourselves breathing in unison.

Suzanne and I are mentally calling forth the angelic doorkeepers, waiting to receive him, and communicating with Kimo's spirit, as he begins to slip into semi-consciousness. Very gently, silently, Prakash arrives to join us. He is quite early, he was not due until later today, he must have felt the timing for Kimo. As he takes Kimo's other hand, Kimo opens his eyes for just a moment. After his acknowledgement and acceptance of Prakash he drifts back into his journey.

Suzanne and I have not had a moment this morning to call Peggy. Even though she is working, she would leave quickly to be here, but Kimo's departure seems to be happening so quickly, we have been caught up in it. Peggy was here last night and many other nights. All she wanted to say or do has been completed. Perhaps it will be a bit less painful this way.

Kimo's breathing slows now and shifts rhythm. The drumming, which is actually air moving through his relaxed mouth, continues to be the only sound. Time is passing around us but not through us, in this other-worldly atmosphere…It feels as though we are floating in a separate time/space. It feels as though we are moving through water.

And then…his breath ceased…calmly, gently…Kimo's body died. I mentally note the time and release his feet.

The three of us sit in silence for what feels like an eternity. Finally, we move from Kimo's bed and hug each other. We sit and share our inner experience for a time. We talk of Kimo and we talk to Kimo, as his body lay still in the bed and his spirit hovers in the room…

John Victor (Kimo) Dela Cruz released his body at 10:15 am November 16, 1992—If his son reads this, please contact me, Jeri, through the publisher.

Two Days Later

Suzanne and I were sitting at my dining table, exhausted from the tasks that follow the death of a loved one. The room was silent as we just stared into space. Suddenly, there was an odd noise. I looked toward the sound, which was coming from the floor next to a desk in the same room. Four bottles of aloe juice, which had been standing upright there for days, were toppled over. I heard Kimo saying, *"See, I told you this stuff wouldn't work."* I said, in reply (aloud), "O.K. big boy, now pick them back up." Suzanne and I stared at the bottles for a while but they didn't move again.

A month ago, when we brought Kimo home from the hospital, I suggested he try the aloe concentrate for it's healing properties. He consumed exactly two doses. He didn't like the taste.

As Suzanne and I stared at the bottles, I remarked that I thought it was the "sign" Kimo said he would give to us.

A Visit With Kimo's Spirit

Three days after Kimo passed away, Roy, Donna and I gathered in "session" to communicate with him. This session was unlike any other session we had done in the course of our work. Most of the discarnates we speak with are strangers. It is very different to speak with someone you were with, in the "physical," just a few days ago.

Roy is the channel for Kimo. Often he will relate what he sees or is being said by Kimo rather than speaking as Kimo directly. Kimo speaking directly, is in bold italics. The following conversation is from the audio tape of that session:

ROY: He hears music, he's singing, he's happy right now, he feels better. He says he doesn't even need to limp. If you look at his body (ethereal), everything is perfect. He is showing himself the same as he was at his earthly age of twenty-three to twenty-seven (this is common with discarnates).

He is very comfortable, very healthy and very happy—although, he doesn't want to stay around in the space he is in too long. Evidently he has some friends that have been there and are helping him…a fellow-musician (Danny), as well as some family. Since you (Jeri and Suzanne) did ceremony before (prior to his death) to ask for guides, he has Archangels Michael and Raphael. He also has a guide named Augustine who is helping him.

Kimo says, "*I never believed the movie, Ghost, but now I believe.*" And yeah, after you told him to try to pick up the bottles, he did try but couldn't. He asked his friend (Danny) to help him but his friend said no, you have to do it. So he was a little embarrassed because he could knock them down but he still hadn't learned how to "lift." His hand kept coming through them…but he says that's not important anyhow.

JERI: No, it isn't. So, you did knock over the aloe bottles, right?

ROY: Yes, trying to get your attention, trying to be silly as well showing you the "sign."

JERI: Well, thank you.

ROY: Also, he says he's sorry if he scared Suzanne last night in the cottage, he was trying to hug her. He says he spent time going through the cottage, looking at things that he held very dear, but realized he needed to let go of them. He cried as he realized that he felt so free and joyous and that he still had the memories of his lifetime, choices he made, choices he didn't make…"*you're right Jeri, if I had made other choices, I would be living today.*"

JERI: Yes, but all is meant to be.

ROY: His biggest concern is that he hasn't hurt any of you or other people (he went on about personal issues)…all he keeps saying is, you're right Jeri, about all the things you have told me about death. He says he wants to share more of what he has been learning, but they (spirit guides) say, "No, not now, they (we) must experience for themselves at the right time."

Kimo says he never understood what love is, or was, when he lived—now he understands what love is. He understands what it is to walk around freely and to be normal again and not have all the earthly worries (he worried a lot). There is no time and you do what you want. Although, he was told that when he goes through that "Lighted Way," there will be other decisions he has to make and things he has to do, duties to perform. He understands but it was confusing to him because he thought when you go to heaven (the Light), it isn't like normal life, but they're telling him it is an expanded view of normal life, a continuum of life. For now, he can walk through doors and through walls and can see through things—and when he wants to recall something in memory, it appears in seconds. When he wants to look at the future of people he loves and who took care of him, he can see it and wants to speak about it, but he can't.

JERI: We understand

DONNA: What about this song I hear him sing? Its "I'm sorry, so sorry...."

ROY: That's an old song. He feels he was a burden, the way he treated people all his life. He sees how much pressure he put on some people and how much burden he put on others because of his own frustration and feeling of worthlessness. He sees he was beating himself up in the end.

JERI: Absolutely, he put pressure and burden on himself even more!

DONNA: So, what was that song he was singing to me while I was out in the garden the other night?

ROY: He says, yes, he wants to let you know that in three lifetimes you were his wife and there was a spark of knowing before he died. After he went through the veil, it was revealed. He asked to "see" about other people in his life and was shown why they were there, regardless of how he treated them. He was shown past karmatic relationships and the role he was playing for them in this life. He cried and asked why it all had to happen the way it did. The guides explained. He understood.

It seems he will be reincarnating to complete a little more unfinished business from this life (now past). He sees so much that he could have done differently, although his reasons were valid at the time. There is a great teacher waiting at the end of the tunnel, beyond the Light.

JERI: Were you comfortable during the deathing process. Did that go well for you?

ROY: He was real scared, *"at the time you saw me looking through the eyes, I was trying to talk to you. I couldn't talk but I heard your mind and what you guys were saying. I wanted to tell you what was happening because it was scary, but exciting and I just needed your love and comfort, which you gave. I wanted hugs but it was not right. They (guides) told me I had to do it myself, that if I used your energies from hugs, it was like clinging on and not letting go, and it would have been more painful."*

JERI: It was enough that we were holding his hands and feet. We didn't want to slow the process for him.

ROY: His concern was his fear. He could see other "beings" that he didn't understand, and those in "life" who were familiar—until he left his body and felt this freedom and release and the love and comfort of the "other beings." Then he understood. After that, each one of you received a hug and a kiss from him and he was crying.

JERI: We felt him.

ROY: You should have heard music.

JERI: Yes, I did.

ROY: He has visited and talked and played with other people.

JERI: Junior (a nephew) remembers your visit the other night, when you told him you weren't dead. He called me. Yes, the first song I heard you sing was, "I've been alive forever, and I wrote the very first song…I write the songs…"

ROY: *"That is what they* (guides) *were showing me—just like you said, I make my own life."*

DONNA: Kimo, do you understand or can you tell us if there was any connection going on between the three of us (Donna, Jeri and Kimo), with that heart pain we all had for a couple of weeks?

ROY: Several times (lives) before, you, Jeri, Suzanne, Peggy and Prakash attended him at his death-bed. Often, it was through deep love and respect. He has also done that for all of you at different times. The pain was the pain of the memories as family losing a loved one, in times where there was just fear and grief, without understanding of the spiritual process of life and death, as you have today.

JERI: Is there anything else I can do to help your family?

ROY: *"Just what you already do. Many had pity and contempt* (for me) *through my life, and now they feel guilty."* His main concern is that arrangements be played out as he requested.

JERI: Yes, it will be done.

ROY: He wants to be released, but he wants to stay for the party on Sunday (four days from now). He wants to eat food and hear music. He will be playing music too, but some will hear and some will not. His time will be limited on Sunday. In the early evening he will be stepping into the Light. *"Jeri, take care of Suzanne and Peggy—you're right about my son, Its up to you if you want to find him. I didn't want to admit, in life, that I loved a lot of things, because it was more painful than joyful."*

DONNA: So, Kimo, how would you describe your feelings at this time?

ROY: *"Totally free—one of the best musicians around."*

JERI: That's right!

ROY: *"My body's renewed, I look like I can have any woman in the world again* (he was very handsome), *I just feel happy and healthy and I just want everybody to know, it's great to be alive! The baggage I left back there looks funny, but you know, it feels so much better to be where I am and I know it will be greater where I'm going. I have a lot of help and protection and it's all due to all of you and what we have been through. When I say I'm sorry, it is for not sharing the joy of the love of life I had, the way it should have been shared."* He (Kimo) is crying.

JERI: I called Danny in as you were departing.

ROY: *"Yeah, Danny is right here and he has been helping me out a lot. He says that he was beyond the Light, but got permission to come back and help me. Danny can't speak right now, he's not allowed to, but he would like everyone to know that everything is O.K. for him and will be for me. In fact, he says it will be great! He says I can have my guitar on the other side too."*

JERI: Yes, I told you you would love it. Your sister asked me for your guitar (the physical one), is that O.K. with you?

ROY: *"I gave everything to you, do what you think is right."*

JERI: I feel she needs to have it. I would like to say hello to Danny and thank him for coming.

ROY: He is glad to have the opportunity to repay kindness from the past. Kimo is saying, *"expect the best and greatest love, there is much awaiting each of you. Danny and I will be visiting all of you in the next few days."* On Sunday, the time will be between 9 and 10 pm for Kimo to step through the light, so if you will all focus your energies again to comfort and guide him...

JERI: Yes, we will do that...we will close for now. We give thanks to all divine beings who are assisting Kimo and Danny as we close this circle with much love.

Kimo gave specific orders for "no funeral, no service, no nothing." Peggy felt that his friends needed the opportunity to come together in some way. Suzanne and I agreed. We also felt that his family needed the ceremony of closure. So, Peggy arranged it and called it the "I Don't Care What You Said Cuz You're Dead" party.

Kimo did not seem to mind at all. The party on Sunday was wonderful, with lots of friends and family sharing memories and lots of food. We had a beach party at, what we always refer to as, "Kimo's Camp." He spent most weekends there and many of us would join him on Sundays, for a playful ritual of sun, food, swimming, relaxing and sharing joys and sorrows.

At sunset, a small group of us left to take Kimo's ashes to complete his departure by burying them under the orchid tree. It had started to rain off and on, so we sat on my porch to wait for a dry spell. The rain continued. As it grew closer to nine o'clock, we were wondering if it would stop at all.

Finally, I asked everyone to join me as I made a "request" (of the gods) for the rain to stop long enough for us to place the ashes. A few of our guests chuckled…until the rain stopped about three minutes later.

We placed the ashes under the tree and called upon Archangel Michael to assist in releasing Kimo into Divine Light…aloha oe, Kimo san…

Transition

Life is continuous and eternal. The soul/spirit exists always, whether or not it is manifest in physical form. We are immortal! Life goes on after death, although we each experience it in our own way. Death is a journey, a transition from one state of consciousness to another, from one level of vibrational frequency to a higher one. There are more soul/spirits in non-physical form than there are in physical form. We the embodied are in the minority!

Our deaths are experienced from our individual perspectives. We each function from our own blueprint created at the soul level which coincides with the Universal Principles. These Principles are the ultimate blueprint for all that exists, animate or inanimate. The Universal Principles are the underlying factors that maintain order in all that Is.

The number of lives we experience does not negate the importance of each and every one. All are for the purpose of experience and learning. Many people have lost touch with their Spirit and are caught up in their mistakes, or pain from sad experiences. Some become very attached to the physical things of earth-life: money, objects, emotions, relationships or habits. Some fear death and don't want to go there because they think it is the end of them or it is going to be hell. It will be if you think so.

There are many negative attitudes that people carry around, such as "no pain, no gain," "life's a bitch and then you die" or "unless you are a member of (fill in the blank) church you'll go to hell." These and other contrary attitudes have accumulated through exposure to negative situations from this and other lifetimes, which are viewed through limited awareness. We need to break out of these attitudes so we can grow in spirit, live in joy (our natural state of being) and leave this plane via a peaceful transition. It is for this reason that I have included tools in this book, to assist you in clearing these negative patterns. All of the tools and processes are described in the Toolbox chapter.

Life on any plane is what WE make it. We choose our lives and deaths (transitions). We choose our births, our parents and environment prior to coming here just as we would choose our classes in college. I have reminded my children of that numerous times. Yes, we have assistance from counselors (spirit guides) as to where, what and when, but we make the final choice.

If we keep sight of each experience as a lesson, every life as a classroom for adventure, and treat EACH ONE as a wonderful opportunity to grow, explore and expand, we give ourselves total power over our own destiny. Then we can enjoy each life to its fullest and learn the ultimate lesson…LOVE.

Experience through relationship, is the classroom—relating to all experience through the understanding of love, is the lesson!

To those left behind, some deaths seem to be senseless tragedies: accidents, suicides, homicides, death in combat, mass transit deaths, natural disasters, a child who seems to have their whole life ahead of them, or a loved one we need and feel we can't live without. All of these situations are individual soul choices usually made for reasons unknown to the survivors. There is a learning experience taking place for everyone involved—those who have died, and those still living. It seems unfair, but we usually do need to walk through the emotional agony of painful earthly situations for our own growth, to be stimulated into improving the quality of the self and our lives as a result of loss and for the completion of karmatic lessons. In any case, I encourage you to call upon Spirit to assist because we don't always have the whole picture of their destiny or ours. Trust that Divine Will is at work.

It is important to alter our negative view of death and beyond and to understand how we can assist in the dying process for each other. Each of us has been or will be affected by death of those around us, and ultimately our own.

We Can Help

We can be of great assistance to a person near death or to a soul who has just passed on. After doing your own personal clearing process, fill yourself with soft, rose pink light (love energy) and surround them in pure white light. Mentally call for Divine Guidance, and ask for assistance, in the form of a safe and peaceful passage.

This is a good time to do the Ho'oponopono process (see Toolbox chapter) if you feel drawn to it. Communicate all that you wish to the dying person. Tell them the things you may have left unsaid up till now—apologies, forgiveness or unexpressed love. Now is the time to cleanse and release for your sake and for theirs. Then, encourage them to do the same with anyone they wish to, or with you. You can then call upon Angelic assistance for them, to recieve them on the other side and give them guidance and protection. Allow and assist a dying person to go, whether you agree with their choice or not.

After you have helped them tend to their affairs you can encourage them to relax and be at peace. You can review pleasant times of the past. You can create a lovely space in their room for them to release—soft music, candles, flowers or plants, fragrance and any other items they might want near them. They might want someone to sing or recite poetry or other material to them. Ask whom they might want to see on the other side. Perhaps they have already seen a loved one, you can speak to that person, asking them to receive them as the dying one passes over.

Sometimes you can't know if someone is going to die or recover. Simply request a healing for them, and trust whatever form it takes. We do not have to understand about their death to be of assistance. For some, death IS their healing. For others, a health crisis is their renewal.

You can also assist a friend or loved one who has recently passed away. This can be helpful, especially, if you have not had the opportunity to see them or talk to them before they died. Perhaps they have come to you in dreams or you have felt their presence. You can choose a quiet time and place for communication with the deceased. You can do it at bedtime before going to sleep. Simply call their name and ask to speak to them. You may or may not feel them there but that is O.K. Proceed to talk to them and complete what you wish to say. Encourage them in the same way that I have described above, for those near death. This will assist them in completing their death journey. When you are finished, release them in Love and Light to the Angelic escorts of Archangel Michael.

The following is part of the eulogy I use when I minister a funeral service:

"Our journey away from this earthly plane can be a far greater experience than our entry into this life, like a reward for many years of study in the earth-school.

As we leave our loved ones behind, we can only hope they do not suffer long from their loss and can rejoice in our graduation, celebrating our rebirth into new life…while patiently knowing of the inevitable reunion, in another time and place.

For true love bonds are never broken."

Twelve Dimensions

In metaphysical terminology, dimension refers to the categorization of measured vibrational frequencies into various levels. ALL that exists has a vibrational rate (frequency, pattern). ALL is in movement, whether it is a living being or an object. Dimensions are not places, but frequencies of existence. The higher the vibratory rate, the less density. A rock has a lower vibrational rate than a tree. A tree has a lower vibrational rate than a human. A human has a lower vibrational rate than an angel, and so on.

Other terms for the dimensions are densities, planes, plateaus, realms or in the bible, mansions. John 14:2 quotes Emmanuel (Jesus) at the last supper. Knowing of his impending death, he said: "In my father's house are many mansions: if it were not so, I would have told you. I go to prepare a place for you." I believe he was referring to the other dimensions beyond this one wherein each of us travels on our journey back to the source (creator).

I will focus on the first twelve dimensions that are commonly referred to by the mystical community. I believe there are probably endless dimensions in a given universe and I wonder if they encompass our entire universe, other universes—are they different in each universe? This chapter is a simplified interpretation of what one might find in the twelve dimensions as related by numerous mystical earthlings, laid out for the purpose of exploring the differences between them. Each person will experience any given dimension in their own way, from their own perspective, just as each person experiences this third dimensional earth-life in their own way. Within the dimensions there are many different levels, just as there are many departments within each university.

ALL sentient beings (human or otherwise) are inter-and multi-dimensional! Many of our inter-dimensional experiences do not register fully into the conscious mind. Dreams and sleep-travel are some examples, as is also the creative imagination (image-nation). The other dimensions are not far away. They are right here, just through the doors of consciousness. The doors are within us.

As we balance our emotional bodies, we expand our awareness. This is essential for safe inter-dimensional travel. For some, this expansion happens as a natural part of evolution. For others who consciously desire to travel, there are many methods to assist in expanding this process. These methods include hypnosis, meditation, and any other form of inner exploration of altered states of consciousness. There is much to do and explore on the "inner planes."

Some prefer to use drugs to traverse other-dimensional worlds. I feel this causes distortion and can draw disharmonious energies or entities to us. I encourage the careful exploration using our mind, which has innate ability, and to work with one's own Spirit Guides for safety. I encourage you to choose the methods that feel right for you. The fact is, we have passed through these dimensions before during our long journey of the soul, and will again as we pass from one life to another. Belief is not required, it is a natural part of our reality.

After the original chaos of planetary creation, Infinite Intelligence begins a spiral journey, a series of vibrational experiences through the many dimensions. This process is that of emergence, exploration, experience, and return. I like to think of it as a safari!

The following information is from my observations and research, and experiences shared with me by many others. I encourage you to consider this information only as a possibility, not as any kind of limitation to what your own observations or experiences may be.

Dimensional Safari

Shall we begin our tour?

FIRST: Linear, flat—moving only in one direction—atomic awareness in physical matter as in water and minerals.

SECOND: Moving with height and width—flat, like a photograph or picture—seeing through only one eye—animal and plant awareness, movement toward growth, Light.

THIRD: Moving with height, width, depth—has gravity and mass which limit time and space—seeing through both eyes. Human self-awareness through separation. Individual intelligence. Earth, as we experience it daily.

FOURTH: The astral—here, relocation is instantaneous in time/space—very interactive with the third dimension—the link between mind and matter (the cause of growth)—movement in all directions. Vibrating at a faster rate, form is of a lesser density than in the third dimension. It surrounds and penetrates Earth, but there is no time or distance, as we know it. There is emotion, but not the usual physical activity of life as we experience it. Awareness of other selves.

The lowest levels of this dimension (sometimes called the Bardo plane) are where there is confusion, negativity, temptation and fantasy. Here, one can find the dark forces, lost or earthbound spirits, and the negative thought patterns (energy) of incarnated humans. One must be very careful if choosing to journey into, or communicate with this level. Many have tapped into this level through the use of Ouiji boards, seances, drugs, alcohol, hypnosis, astral projection and exorcisms (accidentally or deliberately). Many have become attached to or possessed by the dark beings who dwell here.

Moving into various levels of this dimension, one can find Nature Spirits or Elementals. These beings are the lower manifestations of the Angelic Kingdom. They govern the four elements of air, fire, water and earth. They are elements in concentrated forms of energy and can change their appearance. There are hundreds of varieties. Often they take human-like form in miniature like Fairies and Elves, or larger proportions like Pan, Mermaids, Mermen. They can easily manifest into the third dimension, which is the reason for numerous sightings by and interactions with humans. They are governed by the upper Angelic realm, and are often the messengers of the Angels. They can influence human thought and emotion.

It is thought, by some, that Elementals are an early form of human evolution. They can be loving, mischievous, or even dangerous. They respond readily to human emotions—they are unpredictable. They synchronize to the energy at hand and work through and with the patterns of the elements (air, fire, earth, water) of nature. There are also various types of Extraterrestrials in this density. Individuality is retained.

FIFTH: This is the mental/spiritual dimension. Vibrating at a faster rate than the fourth dimension, it also surrounds and permeates the earth. Here, the Devas of the angelic kingdom create and formulate the design of form and activity prior to it's manifestation in the physical/earth density—they are the overseers, the highest level of the Elemental Kingdom—this dimension has been described as heaven by those who have had a near-death experience. It is a reception area for many, once they complete their death journey. Many personal spirit guides emanate from this level. Some Extraterrestrials of higher evolution exist in this dimension. All activity emanates from the spiritual aspect of personality. Individuality is retained in this density.

SIXTH: The source of intuition and wisdom—the source of constructive imagination, where one receives awareness of unconditional love (agape) for humanity—the source of spiritual awareness, discernment and the true nature of reality (as opposed to limited physical reality). The duality of positive and negative polarity begins to dissipate. This is where we can tap into the river of knowledge, a universal source. From here comes the basis of communication through language and music, through the healing arts, astrology, numerology systems and other metaphysical sciences. Individuality is retained and expanded upon.

SEVENTH: Pure spiritual essence. The highest level of separateness where self-realization manifests individuality of spirit/personality, it manifests as pure color and sound. Self-realization begins to manifest from Universal Will. One begins to be unified with the totality of being. The individual spirit begins to function as part of a group, which works for the good of ALL.

EIGHTH: Group spirit. Here spirit manifests as unique group energies. These energies can be called potential social memory complexes and can manifest on the earth plane as groups working together for a common cause, partnerships or other group/team structures. In this dimension the self begins to join others, it expands through group mind/spirit and expresses itself by manifesting in increasingly larger groups. The akashic records of past and future potential exist here.

NINTH: Christ vibration. This dimension could be called bliss or pure Christ-consciousness, Cosmic-consciousness beyond duality. The highest level of pure spirit—pure knowledge—selfless love and compassion in Universal Service. A state where we can experience celestial bodies of planets, stars, galaxies and universes as purposeful conscious beings with spirit and soul—in totality.

TENTH: Buddhic vibration. Divine Wisdom. Universal Love for all humanity, accessed through soul/mind.

ELEVENTH: Masters vibration. The level of Divine Universal Teachers, who can impart Divine Light Teachings to all who will receive them.

TWELFTH: God—Source—That which is complete.

BEYOND:???

The end of our tour…and the beginning…

Universal Principles

The Universal Principles are a set of natural laws encoded within all things and all dimensionalities of the Universe. These principles maintain perfect order in the Universe, which is in a continuous process of balance. The Laws are timeless and unchanging. There are no exceptions, only mis-perceptions of their functioning.

For those who function within these principles, their life moves in a positive progression. For those who move against these principles, their life is a path of difficulty, struggle and suffering. Neither path is wrong or right. All paths are simply experience. The choice of that experience is the privilege of each soul. All paths lead back to the creator/source.

All beings are bound by these Principles, whether they are conscious of them or not, whether they choose to abide by them or not. The consequences of acting contrary to the Universal Principles are self-imposed from a soul/spirit level of understanding. Some refer to them as the Laws of Karma. All of the Universal Principles are interwoven and interrelate with each other.

Many of these principles are addressed throughout this book. The ones listed below are a condensed and combined list pertaining to the most common issues of our earthly lives.

1. THE LAW OF ONE—THE LAW OF EVOLUTION

   All spirit/souls are connected on the higher levels. As we move through our evolution, we affect Every other soul through our thoughts and actions, creating harmony or disharmony.

2. THE LAW OF CONTINUITY

   Nothing, animate or inanimate, ever dies or is destroyed—it simply changes form.

3. THE LAW OF DYING—THE LAW OF REINCARNATION

Once each being or thing accumulates all the knowledge needed from a current mode of existence (lifetime), there is withdrawal from that level, which manifests as a change of form. This accumulation raises the vibrational frequency and one moves into a new mode of existence at a higher vibrational level. This applies to all things animate or inanimate.

4. THE LAW OF KARMA AND KARMIC EXCESS

Divine Justice, is based on the concept that, in the beginning, all are created equal, completely independent and self-responsible. Any thought or action with intent of purpose creates good or bad karmic reaction. What we put out comes back. Rectification is self-imposed from a soul level. When all contrary karmic patterns are cleared, we are released from the cycle of re-incarnation. When there is an excess of harmonious or disharmonious karmic output within one lifetime, the return is absorbed into more than one lifetime. This prevents one from being out of balance. We are never given more than we can handle. The Law of Karma is imposed until Harmony is attained.

5. THE LAW OF WISDOM

Wisdom clears Karma. Making choices through wisdom, eases the pattern of learning though pain and struggle.

6. THE LAW OF GRACE

Forgiveness, of self and others, through unconditional love and mercy, serves the higher good of all. This moves one into the state of Grace which always exists at it's own frequency. As you give, you will receive.

7. THE LAW OF FREE WILL—THE LAW OF COMPENSATION

Everyone has the right of Free Will in all things at all times. It is our Free Will to choose how we respond to everything. Each one of us is responsible for everything that touches us or happens to us. We draw influence and experience to ourselves by our thoughts, from past and/or present lifetimes. Our attitudes dictate our experience, always.

8.   THE LAW OF ABUNDANCE—THE LAW OF PROSPERITY

We each already have access, to whatever we need to create our own abundance here on earth. We choose whether to utilize this access or not.

9.   THE LAW OF SELF-WORTH

We can only attract to ourselves, that which we feel worthy of. Our self-esteem is the gauge to that worthiness. In truth, we are already perfect in this moment. Know the self from a state of Grace.

10.   THE LAW OF SELF-DELUSION—THE LAW OF ATTITUDE

We experience discomfort when our beliefs or actions conflict with themselves or each other. Instinct tells us to eliminate one or the other for relief. Our comfort and safety are governed by our choice of attitude. Our attitude is the only thing that CREATES that which can harm us. We are what we believe.

11.   THE LAW OF DENIAL

When we avoid responsibility for our self and our experiences, discomfort manifests in the body, mind and spirit—until we release our denial. Only then can we be in harmony and health. Each soul/spirit (person) is responsible for what happens to him/her.

12.   THE LAW OF RESISTANCE

That which we fear or resist, we will draw to ourselves. This will continue until we have learned to release the fear.

13.   THE LAW OF ATTRACTION

To that which we are fascinated with is where our energy will go. We attract what we are and what we concentrate upon, be it contrary or harmonious.

14.   THE LAW OF RESTRICTION

We can only create what is equal to our own level of understanding, individually and collectively.

15. THE LAW OF DOMINANT DESIRE

The stronger emotions will always dominate the weaker ones, be they positive or negative. The strongest emotion will bleed into all your actions.

16. THE LAW OF THREES—THE LAW OF TRIANGULATION

There is a triune aspect in all of nature, all things animate or inanimate. When three become a unified whole, it benefits all. This is the basis of manifestation.

17. THE LAW OF REFLECTION

The aspects you respond to in others, you are recognizing in yourself, whether they are harmonious or contrary. We are reflections for each other.

18. THE LAW OF GRATITUDE

The more we give, the more we receive. As we give with integrity and clear intent of right action, we will receive the same in return.

19. THE LAW OF EVOLUTION—THE LAW OF PERFECTION

All that exists, animate or inanimate, has a purposeful vibration, guided by innate intelligence. Each is self-guided to fulfill a specific purpose. Upon completion, each moves into a higher vibration. This pattern exists in All things. All things are in the process of returning to perfect balance at all times.

20. THE LAW OF DOMINION—THE LAW OF SURVIVAL

God/Man intentionally co-create by thought. Thought which is linked into infinite intelligence existing in all matter/energy. To think is to create, be it contrary or harmonious. Mankind co-creates, individually and collectively, all that is in the Universe! As long as the soul/mind of humanity desires earthly (physical) experience, it will be.

21. THE LAW OF IMAGINATION

Imagination is the most powerful source to change ideas and beliefs for human improvement. "If imagination comes in conflict with willpower, willpower will always lose" (June Bletzer). "Imagination is more important than knowledge" (Albert Einstein).

22. THE LAW OF GOOD—THE LAW OF LIGHT

All that is, is good or of Light. There is no evil in reality, only a system of the polarity of opposites, most evident in lower dimensional planes. There is no sin, only experience. There is no death, only rebirth. All else is opinion or judgement.

The Deceased

People who have died still exist in other dimensions. They are still "living" but they are without a physical body. A common term for them is "discarnate." The word discarnate means "without flesh or meat" or bone...ie: dis-embodied. This describes all humans (the soul-mind) who have had one or more lifetimes on planet earth. Another common term for a discarnate or other astral or ethereal being is "entity." I will use both of these terms to refer to the deceased.

Some people complete their death journey easily. They are receptive and have assistance from their Spirit Guides and/or deceased loved ones who are tending their process. They usually have loved ones (embodied) who are assisting their passing from "this side" as well. They have an acceptance about the nature of death. They have settled their affairs & are at peace with their journey. Others have difficulty, confusion or great prolonged suffering in their passing from this world to the next. This can be caused by many factors including sudden death, suicide, strong negative emotional patterns, loved ones holding on, a feeling of unfinished business, unwillingness to let go of physical pleasures or a very fearful and distorted attitude about death. When this happens, they can get stuck in their process and/or detained in the lower astral realms where these same negative energies abound. "Like attracts like" and it is no different there. It is also referred to as the 4 th dimension or the Bardo Plane. Often, they have been carrying discarnates with those similar negative patterns, attached to them from some part of their lifetime. The dying person simply joins them in the astral, at the time of death.

Astral Inhabitants—Our Neighbors

In the astral realm there is awareness of past, present and future. Entities there have various degrees of access to this information depending on their level of understanding and maturity.

There can be a "bleed-through" from that dimension to this one where some form of contact is made with those embodied (the living). This contact has been perceived by many people, through one or more of their physical senses (sight, sound, smell and touch). Contact can also be made through your psychic or intuitive senses.

Unfortunately, there are many types of mental health therapists who obtain information from their patient/client that is actually not pertaining to the patient/client themselves, but astral entities—even in hypnosis, when the patient is relating what they see or hear or feel, it can be the actual experience or information from a discarnate human or other astral being which is obtained. However, hypnosis can provide easy access to these astral realms and assist in communication with any of the entities that may be attached to a patient/client.

I encourage this be taken into consideration by all practitioners of the healing arts, especially in cases of supposed abuse by others. Who has been abused? The patient in body—or the discarnate in attachment to the patient? Think about it. There is a BIG difference, especially when you plan to confront and accuse the supposed perpetrator(s)! This is especially true in cases where the patient has had any experience with extraterrestrial abduction involving medical experiments on their body. These experiments can seem like sexual or physical abuse, or even a kind of satanic ritual abuse. Many abductees have reported sexually abusive experiences, including rape. This abuse can be blamed on innocent family members or others, simply because very few practitioners acknowledge the reality of discarnate or extraterrestrial interaction with earth humans and still fewer have experience in treating the subsequent trauma.

The idea of contact with ghosts can be very frightening to people who are not aware, or are uncomfortable with this subject. This aversion is usually caused by exposure to misinformation. There is little clear information given about discarnates, even by those who have knowledge or experience. Most people have an attitude of fear about ghosts and about death itself.

This fear can also be connected to guilt about living. This refers to the survivors of the deceased who have unfinished business with those who have passed on, or who are dealing with a pattern within themselves of unworthiness in general. Those who function from a base of guilt and fear will react to the unknown with guilt and fear. Many of our clients are dealing with departed loved ones from present-life, who are stuck in some negative emotional patterns.

One example is a mother who died at age eighty-four and after two years, was still hanging around one of her children. The mother was an alcoholic and the child, now an adult, had terrible resentment, which was caused by the various distortions in the behavior of the mother. The child felt neglected and emotionally abused by her, not mothered in a positive way. The mother was filled with guilt about the kind of mother she wasn't. In the clearing process, both were shown the reality of the situation and agreed to forgiving each other for all harm done. The mother agreed to release.

This case is a good example of the healing that can happen, even after death, for the deceased and the survivors. Those negative patterns, carried by both mother and child, were cleared away by apology and forgiveness through understanding—not to be repeated in this lifetime or the next by either person.

I personally feel that the presentation of information about ghosts should begin with and be taught to the very young, as children are usually very sensitive to beings of other realms and see or communicate with them more often than adults realize. This sensitivity is often suppressed by disbelieving adults who think the child has an overactive imagination. Many children and sensitive adults suffer because of the ignorance and disbelief surrounding this subject.

Indigenous peoples all over the world have a very expanded awareness of "spirits." This information is taught from childhood as a natural and important part of living. The Yuit Eskimos erect spirit poles by the graves to keep the spirits of the dead from disrupting the world of the living. In a book titled, *The Native People of Alaska* by Steve Langdon, he tells of their spiritual philosophies.

"Yuit religious belief systems were heavily influenced by two basic notions. The first of these was that human success in hunting depended on maintaining a positive relationship between people and the spirits of the animals hunted. Amulets, taboos and other ritual activities were designed to show respect to those animal spirits in order to insure continued availability.

The second principle was that of reincarnation, or the cycling of life. It was believed that human spirits were recycled into life through birth and naming. Those who had not been reborn lived in the underground, but occasionally could appear above ground. It was necessary to be vigilant and not offend these spirits since they could bring harm."

May I suggest to you, that this is a general truth about all 'spirits.'

Contact

Spirit contacts are commonly known as hauntings or poltergeist activity. There have been many movies dealing with these situations: *Poltergeist, Ghostbusters, Beetlejuice, Always, Ghost, Casper, What Dreams May Come* and *Practical Magic* to name a few. These are examples of film dramatizing reality, often in a charming and humorous way. Recently, there has been an increase in the number of films, television programs and books dealing with this subject. I feel this reflects the larger population's need to know about these issues, which correlates with an increase in this type of contact activity in general. People are looking for answers to questions they were afraid to ask before. Our planetary vibration is accelerating, creating more of an overlap of the third and fourth dimensions. In people, it is also creating more sensitivity to and awareness of these higher frequencies. This is part of our current planetary evolution.

Another Type Of Contact

A different type of contact comes through "ancestor worship," also referred to as "animism." The most frequent cases we see are the Japanese, Chinese and Hawaiian cultures. These ancestral deities and elder family members are given great respect and acknowledgement. Their honor is always a consideration in making choices in earthly life issues. The Buddhists, Hindus and other religions acknowledge the reality of reincarnation, validating the concept of life after death and that the deceased elders continue to assist the family from beyond as benevolent spirit guides.

Many Japanese have an ancestral altar in their home, called a Butsudan. Daily ritual is performed and offerings are placed at the altars. This practice literally holds the deceased ancestors earthbound, attaching to one or more family members. In Africa, the Masai people believe that those of the other-dimensional worlds control all who are in the physical world (there is a strong probability of truth to this). Their priests consult the spirits for all the important issues of living. One rule for living is that any disharmony between tribal members must be rectified for the good of all (as in Huna tradition). The status of the embodied individuals of the tribe depends on their relationship with the deceased ancestors.

In our communication with the ancestors of our clients, and our own, there are those discarnates who do complete their journey into the "Light" and choose to become spirit guides or guardians for their earthly family. In Hawaiian, these ancestors are referred to as "Aumakua." This arrangement is made through the higher consciousness of the soul connection between all parties involved, whether the Aumakua is for an individual or a whole family.

Traditionally, the Aumakua are called upon to assist in making important decisions or participating in ceremony and ritual. This includes the Ho'oponopono process, the naming of children and the "receiving" of a dying loved one into the next dimension. In general, they are advisors and protectors. There can also be animal Aumakua, which is representative of one or more ancestral connections to that specie or to a Hawaiian deity, which is represented by one or more animals.

When we work with the deceased of these cultures, we encourage all earthbound astral entities to complete their death journey. This includes a form of an orientation and advisory session assisted by Angelic or other Spirit Guides of the higher realms. We ask guidance if it is right timing for the discarnate's release. We share information with them about possible future choices, and that after taking care of their own completion, they may return (in spirit form) to assist loved ones or family. Some are fearful of leaving their family unguarded or without their guidance. We call upon Angelic guides to assist until they return, if they choose to. We honor all gods and goddesses of all cultures, of course, and their representatives.

Those Hawaiians (past and present) who practice Huna (hoo-nah), acknowledge the concept of reincarnation and there is the understanding that the deceased have their own individual life cycles to follow. The heirs often recognize the rebirth of an ancestor in their children or grandchildren. There is also the understanding that "elder souls," who have completed all of their earthly life cycles, can remain as a spirit guides or go on to other levels of existence.

Each of us has a personal individual journey and a more expanded journey with a group of other souls. A soul group can be one's family, business associates, several good friends of many years, a group like ours (as described in the Introduction part of this book) or a group of people who endure a crisis or even perish together. We all are traveling both journeys, weaving the encounters into our collective experience. It is like an incredibly complex tapestry of growth and perfection, and each of us is a single thread. Each thread is a connection to another and so on. The "picture" is awesome!

In past Hawaiian culture, a loved one might keep some of the bones of their deceased loved one or family member, to aid them in continuing to maintain their connection and devotion. Today, the laws prevent that practice in this country. In China, many heirs still wash the bones of their dead once a year. There are some Japanese who wash the body of their dead loved one before it is processed for burial. In Hawaii there are many family graveyards on the residential properties of family that are maintained by the heirs.

The Hawaiian ancestors are always respected. The pantheon of Hawaiian deities is also considered to be ancestors, and the original family line to all Hawaiians. Today, many shrines (heiaus) honoring various deities exist and are well cared for by the people. Ceremonies are often performed, openly or secretly, and offerings are given.

In reality, we all have ancestor spirit guides, whether the ancestors are from our present life lineage or past life. Sometimes, the lineage is one and the same.

What To Do?

When the living encounter unsolicited contact from the dead it can be rather scary or confusing or even traumatic. There can be an inquiry made as to who they are and what they want. If you wish to try this yourself you can. The way to speak to ANY being, including the deceased or unconscious, is simply by talking—mentally or aloud. When talking mentally to an entity that speaks another language, simply request automatic translation. I recommend a quick Ho'oponopono process (see Toolbox chapter) between your three selves and a request for guidance. You can call upon the assistance of Archangel Michael & ask for protection. Then, do the process between yourself and the discarnate being(s) before doing anything else.

We were called to assist a young boy, ten years of age. He would ride his bike through a park each day on his way to and from school. As he rode through the park, he felt a malevolent energy, which frightened him. I told the boy he could call upon Archangel Michael to come and protect him in the park, or any other time he felt a dark presence. I told him that Archangel Michael has a predominant color energy that is a beautiful saphire blue. I suggested that if he forgot the name he could simply call in the "big blue angel" and he would be there. The boy has had peaceful journeys since.

Discarnate Messengers

Perhaps, the discarnate is a loved one, offering guidance or comfort. You might thank them, wish them well and remind them of the opportunity they have to move on. There are some interesting stories of helpful discarnates in the book, *Harper's Encyclopedia of Mystical & Paranormal Experience*, by Rosemary Ellen Guiley. One describes the case of R-101, a British dirigible (blimp) that was destroyed on her maiden voyage in 1930. It sailed from London and crashed in France.

The famous medium, Eileen J. Garrett had premonitions prior to the flight and tried to warn the navigator and Sir Sefton Brancher, the director of civil aviation. Garrett had received the information in two ways. One was in visions and the other was in a seance in 1928, two years prior to the flight. During the seance, a deceased friend of the navigator came through with a warning not to go on the voyage of R-101. Both men rejected the information and the tragic fate of that flight is now history.

Along the same lines, a deceased homicide victim can often tell what really happened to them. The deceased in a supposed suicide can verify if it was suicide, homicide or accidental. This information, although not admissible in court, can be very helpful for the loved ones to understand what really happened and aid in their healing process. We have many cases where the discarnates have provided information that the client would not have otherwise known. There are situations where there is business that is unfinished at the time of death, which can be completed. You can assist the entity in resolving these issues and then encourage them to move on.

Sometimes communication simply provides for personal completion between people, both in and out of body, who have things to say to each other. This communication can alleviate any remaining guilt, anger or fear which can "hold" an entity earthbound. The unresolved issues and emotions can hold an entity earthbound indefinitely, denying that soul/spirit the opportunity to continue his journey and draining the energies of the "host" to whom he/she is attached to through these unresolved issues.

Another situation that may require assistance on the part of an embodied person is one where there is contact from a discarnate who is very confused and who may not yet realize they are dead. This can occur in cases of suicide, sudden death, drug overdose, combat death, etc. Some of these discarnates can be very angry. They may attempt to scare, torment or even harm people. Call upon Archangel Michael to give you protection and assistance. If you feel uncomfortable or frightened by the energy of the discarnate, I urge you to enlist a practitioner to assist.

If you are in a situation where you do feel comfortable and safe with the discarnate energy, you can offer assistance by explaining to them that they are dead. Encourage them to locate the Light and call upon angelic escorts to help them release into that Light.

This process can include explaining that the Divine Light is a doorway where they can find the assistance of their spirit guides and/or deceased loved ones. Inform them that they can find relief from their confusion, their anger, or their pain. Invite them to go into the Light with the angelic escorts. This can also be done in the name of Christ, God, or other similar being of your preference.

Preparation

The ideal mode for this type of assistance is that it be done with care and caution in regard to your emotions. First use a clearing process for yourself that lets you feel centered and detached from fear, anger or sorrow. In this way, you are serving from your highest level of emotional balance. In addition to the "Ho'oponopono Process Between Your Three Selves," we use the "Light Invocation" (see Toolbox chapter) to raise our vibration or frequency, which automatically expands our level of awareness and access to the higher realms. We then call upon Archangel Michael to assist.

Things That Go Bump In The Night

Hauntings are usually caused by discarnates, attached to a building or land. They may resent its use by the embodied and try to move them off "their" property. These beings may require a firmer mode of communication. If you encounter this situation in your own home, place of business or other location you are connected to, the following steps can be taken. Remind them they are deceased. You must make it clear that you will not be moved away and that it does not serve the entity to remain. Assure them that the property will be cared for with respect (and mean it). Firmly encourage them to move on with an offer of assistance in a ceremony of release. In cases where the discarnate is angry or dangerous, I suggest you consult a practitioner to do the clearing.

Sometimes there are those discarnates who desire to stay. Often it is simply not right timing for them to be released. With these entities, we ask that they try to understand and be tolerant of the lack of awareness of the embodied humans they encounter. Most people in the physical world do not "see" spirits and there is a lot of fear and superstition surrounding the entire issue of ghosts. We ask that they remain peaceful. In return, we offer to be respectful and to assist them in the future, should they wish to be released.

One of the services we perform is a cleansing/blessing of land, house or business for owners or tenants. If this process were done at the beginning of every new venture, hauntings would not have to occur. In Hawaii, it is common practice to have this type of ceremony done for vehicles, businesses, houses, vessels, other objects or land. This is because of the knowledge that has been passed down through families about discarnate ancestors and their interaction with the living. Native Americans and other indigenous peoples around the world have ceremonies for this purpose as well.

Whenever we are clearing land, with or without buildings, we call upon Archangel Michael. There are usually many spirits to release from the deaths of those who died there in past times, especially on a piece of land that has been inhabited for generations. Another consideration is that today, the size of a piece of land may be small compared to all the land it may have been connected to before it was subdivided and sold off in pieces. With some clearings there are hundreds of spirits that are released. Those who are sensitive can see the spirits of people and animals rise up and away with the assistance of the Angelic realm. Entire neighborhoods can be cleared in one ceremony with Archangel Michael's assistance by requesting the vortex be expand as far as is permitted. This can reach a larger area covering previous extended boundaries.

One exception to releasing beings is when they are Guardians of specific area. This is common here in Hawaii. In these cases you can request their help identifying undesirable energies. But realize, the Guardians will usually stay with the land, unless they request your assistance for their release. They can be of benefit to the land and the people there as long as the area is treated with respect. An offering of food, flowers, or other plants is made to show respect for them and the land. Some Guardians have been with the land or structure for centuries. Honor them, respect them, work with them and when in doubt, ask!

A Very Bumpy Case

One client of ours was a young girl in a big house with other young people. She and one other girl were familiar with metaphysics and sensitive to energy. I was asked to do a routine blessing because they were new tenants. There were no known disturbances at that time.

During the ceremony, we noticed that there were spirits interfering with the process. This manifested as an attempt to push me down the stairs followed by their successful attempt to knock the bowl of salt water from my hands. I reinforced my own personal clearing and completed this part of the ceremony. I realized this property required a full clearing before a blessing. I called in Archangel Michael to create a large vortex for mass release, as the original size of the land was extensive. During the next few days, all the young people were unnerved by knocking sounds and flashing lights, which so frightened them that they considered moving out. This was an effort at intimidation by the entities and it is common when they are in resistance to a clearing.

During the initial ceremony, we became aware of the presence of two Guardians. The Guardians attempted to communicate with the two girls. One girl clearly received a vision of the Guardians beckoning them to stay, that it would be safe.

I requested the assistance of three other group members who often do this type of work with me. Three days later we successfully completed the clearing.

We thanked and acknowledged the Guardians by planting "Ti" plants around the house. Ti plants are considered to be sacred and are often used in ceremony in Hawaii.

This situation was a very significant reminder for me of the importance of preparation, and a confirmation that there is no such thing as routine ceremony. I had prepared in haste and was emotionally preoccupied with personal matters, which I allowed to interfere with my ability to tune-in to the situation. Had I been clear, I would have known that the situation required a clearing process, not simply a blessing ceremony. This was one of our early cases in our experience with this type of process and we learned that it is best not to work alone when clearing buildings or land

However, there are no accidents…It was an educational experience for the young people, as they observed the physical manifestation of other-dimensional beings. They also learned about communication with and assistance from those beings.

Monsters

Another kind of haunting, can be caused by "monsters." In times past, it was common for sorcerers, using concentrated negative thought forms to create all forms of monster-like creatures. They did this to expand their power and control over those they wished to dominate or torment. It is similar to gathering an army of slaves to work or do battle for it's leader. The biggest army has the most power. Many had the ability to access other-dimensional worlds to capture beings to do their bidding. Dragons and other animal creatures are from these realms. There are many varieties of beings in those worlds and most of them look very scary to humans. In Hawaii, these practitioners are called "Spirit Catchers." They usually capture and use the deceased spirits of humans and animals. We have found that curses often involve the use of these enslaved spirits and creatures to torment the intended prey. Many practitioners continue to use this method today in various parts of the world.

A common problem is the monster-type of nightmares of human children. The forms or beings that children see are usually real. Unfortunately, most parents think it is a fantasy. When a child is sick, perhaps with a high fever, they often see these things and the doctors usually chalk it off to the fever. Yes, some monster images are just projections of fear creating a distortion of an image. One child's monster is another child's pet!

Childhood monsters need to be validated by the caretakers—otherwise, that child's reality is being rejected by those very people who could help them. Any of you could help by first validating the event, stay with the child and say a prayer or make a statement to "whatever" it is, that they must go away and leave this child alone. Say it in the name of Jesus, Buddha, Mohamed or any persona of your preference. Call in Archangel Michael, who is not connected to any religion but scary beings are his specialty.

Ask for Divine protection for the child. Fetch some salt from the kitchen (take the child with you) and sprinkle it in a circle around the bed and put some under the mattress. In Hawaii we use Ti leaves also. We wrap wet salt in the leaf, tie it with some string and put in the child's clothing or under the pillow. You can smudge with sage, cedar or eucalyptus. If the child wishes it, you can stay and sleep the rest of the night with him/her. The fear is real, the event is real! We do clearings in many cases for children and most are quite able to see beings from other dimensions.

In one tragic case, a young boy, age nine, would frequently tell his family of his nightmares. His stories were not given much attention until it was too late. We were called to do an inquiry and a clearing, but only after the boy was found dead from mysterious causes, at the age of ten. We discovered that a horrible curse was put upon him, by some very powerful practitioners from a Melanesian culture.

The energy of the curse continued to plague the remaining family, who described a large gorilla-type creature, dragging a three-foot penis across the windowsill as he made a quick exit from their home. Needless to say, I hear many incredible tales. In this case, I almost lost all composure as this one was being told to me, over the phone, by a very alarmed friend of their family. Fortunately, after many years as a crisis counselor in the field of the paranormal, I am always mindful that the experience of the client is a reality for them and must be treated accordingly.

Yes, we did the clearing and found the "gorilla" to be a shape-shifter, an other-dimensional entity who did the bidding of the practitioners. And fortunately, the curse was lifted before any more harm came to the other members of the family.

The Reluctant Dragon

In another severe case we dealt with a dragon entity, which had been created by a curse maker. The dragon lived in a Chinese woman's home as part of that curse. The curse had been put upon her grandfather, many years ago, and his entire family, for all eternity. The reason for the curse was professional jealousy. In present time, something had stimulated the curse energy to be active. Often, the reactivation is because it is the right timing for a release. Some environmental causes for stimulation include new construction in the area, earthquakes or severe storms with lightning. A human cause can be changes or trauma in the emotional or physical condition of the person(s) involved.

The client was very elderly and was put on drugs for hysteria. She could see the dragon and her fear created great stress for her family. One of her daughters believed what she was saying and asked us for help, so we scheduled a clearing.

The morning of the clearing, the mother called her daughter and said, "No need do the clearing, the house burned down." As the daughter questioned her mother, the daughter realized it was the dragon who burned the house down, in the astral plane, as seen by her elderly mother. We went ahead with the clearing that evening.

When we asked the dragon if he wanted to be released he was very glad. He did not like his "master," the curse maker, but was forced to do his bidding. We released the dragon and the curse maker, separately.

Some people see various monsters or strange-looking organisms when they visit the lower astral plane, especially if the visit is made via the use of mind-altering substances or under emotional stress during sleep. The astral plane is filled with many varieties of creatures, some of which are often seen in movies.

Monsters can be carried over from past lives. Some earth-humans were incarnated as part animal, part human at certain times in history. Mythology books are filled with many "realities" that simply require comprehensive interpretation. These creatures can be dealt with in the same manner as other discarnates.

If you are troubled by scary anomalies, ask your spirit guides, minister or priest to advise you and look into the source of the cause for clarification. To clear it, begin with an evaluation of your physical health and any nutritional suppliments, plant remedies, drugs (including medical prescriptions) or alcohol you may be ingesting. With many of these substances, the quality or dosage, or combinations of them, can affect one's mental perception in sleep or in an awakened state. Next, explore a spiritual cause. Call upon your Higher Guidance to assist you. When in doubt, enlist the services of a practitioner.

It is time to re-awaken our awareness of the influences that the non-physical realms of the deceased, or others, can have upon our lives…the lives of those we love…the lives of those we battle with…the lives of those we work with…the lives of those who live near us…the lives of those who care for and teach our children…etc.

We must also become aware of that influence before we near the end of our lives, as we encounter our own death journey into those realms and beyond.

Possession

○ ○

Plato observed: *"There are many fair things in the life of mortals, but in most of them there are, as it were, adherent keres (spirits of the dead) which pollute and disfigure them."*

The term "possession" is rather intense but it is the most common term used for a deceased (or other) spirit who is attached to or haunting a person, a place or an object of any proportion. We use the word attachment in most cases, as it is a more accurate description of the more common situation of discarnate presence.

The possessing or attaching spirits are of numerous varieties and have been referred to by many names: deceased, disembodied, entities, ghosts, boogies, demons, spirits, spooks and more. It is our experience that these beings exist in various levels of the fourth dimension, the astral plane (see Twelve Dimensions chapter). This plane is sort of "next door" to our physical plane. They are our neighbors!

The terms I will use here for the astral inhabitants are discarnate, entity, spirit or being. The type we will address here are earth humans who are deceased, but earthbound. I specify because not all beings in the Spirit world are deceased. Angels, elementals and many other-dimensional beings are without physical bodies, but are not deceased.

"Full Possession" is a condition where a discarnate means to manipulate and control the host completely. Some discarnates have that motivation, while others are just looking for safety or comfort or something familiar. Some are lost and confused and looking for help. It is simply a matter of the motive on the part of the discarnates in residence and the degree of influence on the individual or situation. They are all attached but only some of them intend or accomplish partial or full possession.

Earthbound discarnates often show themselves and/or communicate with embodied humans. They are often unaware of their physical death and current condition. Their personalities are as varied as those of us in body. Some are more willful than others. Some move around freely, others attach to a location or person who is still in a body (incarnate). Then there are those who go from place to place or person to incarnate person. The semantics of this subject can be confusing. ALL beings are living, so I prefer to honor ALL life. The terms living and dead are not comfortable for me, nor are they accurate, so I will refer to incarnate people as embodied, hosts, earthlings or physical.

Attachment

Partial or complete attachment to a host by one or more entities can and does occur often. This attachment can be born from the desire of spirits to feed on the negative habits and emotions of the host that are similar to their own. Another cause is when the confusion and fear of the entity compels them to be attracted to a person who feels safe to them. Many spirits are not aware they have died. Often, we are the ones who inform them of that reality as we are in a clearing process. Others seek company or a friend, a common situation with hosts who are children or others with a sensitive and compassionate nature. These same hosts often see or feel the entities and invite them consciously or unconsciously. Many discarnates are simply attracted to the Light that a host carries, mistaking that Light for the doorway to heaven.

There are situations where the discarnate and the host know each other or are related. In these cases there are personal karmic reasons for the connection. We encountered an Irish male discarnate, attached to a woman who was often entertained, as were her friends, by the humorous entity. He was also a bit of a trickster and eventually the woman had to do a serious "letting go" of the cheeky little dude.

Those who are researching their own or others' genealogy can also be affected as they are opening up ancestral names and issues. These karmic ties can lie latent until triggered by events, people, situations or information. All names carry the vibration of their owner and we all have some unsavory ancestors in our lineage.

Today, re-incarnation is accepted by most people, and there are volumes written on the subject, including the research of verification. Edgar Cayce gave over two thousand personal readings past-life situations were related to his client's current incarnations. There are those who do not believe in life before or beyond this one. I am not here to prove anything to you. I am addressing this subject because of the many discarnates who are attached to a currently embodied person from a past-life situation. This situation is common with many of our clients and their stories are included in this book.

An example of past "agreement" attachment was a case in which we encountered a Native American Medicine Man who was connected to his apprentice (our client) from a past life.

They had a working agreement in that lifetime of teacher/student, and when the Medicine Man was shot and killed, he attached to the body his apprentice as he vacated his own. He continued to function through the apprentice, drawing life-force energy from her. The apprentice did not cancel the agreement, even after reincarnating. Our client was not consciously aware of any agreement until we discovered the situation during the clearing session.

Another example comes from a client who, in a past life, was the wife and apprentice of a sorcerer/wizard. She was accidentally killed during one of his experiments. As far as he was concerned, her death changed nothing. He considered her his possession.

I asked the client if she wanted him to remain attached. This is a necessary routine question. She very emphatically said NO! This made the wizard husband very angry with both of us. I then called upon escorts from Archangel Michael and the wizard husband was placed into containment where his energies were subdued so we could talk with him. After reasoning with him about the reality of his situation, he became very emotional. He realized he needed to complete his death journey and was released…into the Light.

This guarded containment was very necessary because the wizard initially refused to let go or go into the Light. He enjoyed his experiments and did not want to make any changes. He had been manipulating the wife emotionally and depleting her physically. By saying "no more," she was terminating the original (ancient) agreement.

These kinds of situations are always healed and cleared by invoking the Ho'oponopono Process. If we don't clear the karmatic "contracts," the discarnates can re-attach. You could call that re-possession. In fact, there is a funny movie with that same title and it is about spirit possession. In our line of work we consider these karmatic contracts to be a "legal" issue within the codes of Universal Law (also referred to as Divine or Cosmic Law). Is there such a thing? Absolutely! It explains many things that make no sense otherwise (see Universal Principles chapter).

In many situations, the discarnate is a stranger. They are "picked up" at a particular location during emotionally or physically stressful circumstances experienced by the host. A common situation is when a person is hospitalized, imprisoned or enters a substance abuse treatment center where discarnates have been deposited by a prior host who has had a successful healing or those who have actually died there themselves. Many doctors and nurses are susceptible to attachment due to the nature and locations of their work.

There can be many situations where discarnates desire to connect to an embodied human. These include discarnate addicts of substances who wish to continue their addiction by attaching themselves to a host addict, an angry/violent entity who is drawn to manifest this behavior through a host with similar patterns, a loved one who doesn't want to let go of this world or a particular person, a young entity who seeks shelter and safety…the examples are many.

Another situation is where one discarnate attaches to another discarnate, such as: a child to an adult, a weaker personality to a stronger one, or a group of souls who died together. We have encountered groups of deceased souls in cases of plane crashes and other disasters where many or all were killed. We always ask our own Divine Guidance if our assistance is required to offer protection or release in events of such tragedies that are reported in the news.

Locations

There is a long list of certain locations where attachment can happen more easily for obvious reasons: hospitals, morgues, graveyards, prisons, battlefields or war zones (new or old), any scene of homicidal, suicidal or accidental death, bars, drug and alcohol treatment centers, and so on.

There are other, less obvious locations, places where we have lived or died "before," in past lives. I will give an example. A middle aged couple went to Jamaica for a holiday which was actually a reward issued by the wife's employer for maximum sales of their product for that year. When the couple returned from their trip the wife called me, she was very concerned about her husband's behavior. He had been like "Jekyll & Hyde" since they returned including violent behavior, which was not in his nature at all. We made an appointment and completed a clearing. The husband returned to normal behavior.

In the clearing, it was revealed that a discarnate had attached to the husband at a particular location in Jamaica. The discarnate was a sort of witch doctor, a very tall man who was an adversary from a past incarnation. He believed the husband owed him for a wrong done to him from that prior life. We did the appropriate processes, the husband asked for forgiveness, and the witch doctor reluctantly complied. He agreed to be released into the Light after I told him he would have access to full self-empowerment (which is true, although not self-empowerment in the form that he was familiar with).

In another case we did a clearing on a metaphysical bookstore located in the southern part of the U.S. It was in an old building with a basement. During this long-distance clearing we encountered several discarnates whose bodies were buried in the basement. They were murdered several years prior. It was revealed that this building was a meeting place of the well-known racist cult, and these deaths were part of those activities. Shortly after the clearing, the owner, who had requested our services, told us a large box was left on her doorstep. The box was full of items that were part of the inventory of the store. There was a note attached which stated that these were items stolen from the store and that the author of the note had an overwhelming desire to bring everything back. A very nice surprise and an example of how extensive a clearing/healing can be.

Even we, as exorcists, require clearing sometimes. I will share a personal experience, which happened to me on the island of Kauai while I was conducting a wedding ceremony. Even though it was a working trip, five other members of our group joined me there and we stayed a couple of days just for fun.

The wedding took place on the grounds of a hotel located on a very large bay. In this life I had never been to that area before. As we walked near the shore I was very moved by the beauty of the scene. Then the scene began to change to another time. As I stood there, feeling a warm familiar wave of energy, I saw a large bustling village all along the shoreline with native people going about their daily activities. There were ancient dwellings and canoes, some in the water, others up on shore. I remarked to Suzanne, "I have been here before, this was home."

The memory faded as someone called for me to begin the service for the wedding. I had to compose myself emotionally and separate from that lifetime. I completed the ceremony and we all had a wonderful time at the reception. Then we changed our clothes and went off to play.

Two days later, at home on Maui as I was unpacking, a huge centipede fell out of the dress I had worn for the ceremony. I was very startled and asked my husband, Reuben, to capture the many-legged one. As he did that, I wondered what message the creature was bringing. We normally never have centipedes, as our house is raised above the ground. Traditionally, they represent a situation of jealousy. Reuben made a comment about it and I said, "Yes, I will tune in to this."

We discovered a discarnate who was my brother from that past life. He was very jealous of me in that life because I had been given a position in the village that he had wanted for himself. He made an attempt on my life and was killed for it. He blamed me for his death and held it against me. Another one of those "political things." I am glad I found him so we could complete with forgiveness and release him.

Basically, the entire planet is full of deceased people (and animals) from the past. It is a good practice to tread carefully in any new location where you have not been before in your present lifetime. It is also a good idea to pay your respects to the ancestor spirits of any new ground you enter. You could have some old business there.

Sacred Ground

There are many sites all over this planet that are sacred or coveted by someone. These can be sites of burial, worship, sacred pathways, or storage for treasured objects or records. These sacred locations are usually from past civilizations. Energies that were intentionally placed or spirits can become suspended there for centuries. The place of death or burial of anyone can be considered sacred ground. Death, like birth, is a sacred event in each life. For this reason, it is important to clear locations of death, including scenes of battle or accident, by releasing the spirits of those deceased who may be stuck there.

Situations of potential danger exist in these locations for those in body. A vortex (concentration of specific energy) can manifest from the emotional intensity of the entity's experience. In the astral plane time, as we know it, does not move forward. Violent energy can linger at the site for years after an incident and create mishap or tragedy for those in body who pass by or through the site.

Some sacred sites are deliberately sealed with protection in the form of an energy vortex and/or actual Spirit Guardians are bound there to keep intruders out. Some of these protective energies can remain active for centuries, depending on the force with which they were activated. One example of these protective energies is the tomb of the pharaoh Tutankhamun. Many have told of the tragedies affecting those involved in the discovery and opening of his tomb. Discarnate Spirit Guardians can remain bound to an area and active for centuries as well. Sometimes Guardians were chosen from embodied humans, given their instructions, and then ceremonially killed or buried alive. These discarnates would follow their orders on into the astral plane. The invocations were often issued "for all eternity!"

There are many sacred sites here in Hawaii. The Hawaiian word is heiau (hay-ee-ow). Some people stumble into them unaware of possible consequences. One female visitor experienced such an ordeal. After entering a sacred area she began to become disoriented and started to babble in an old Hawaiian dialect. Her companions were alarmed and took her to our only hospital (Maui Memorial). The medical team was confused and she was placed in the psychiatric unit. I don't know what became of her. The story was related to me by a friend of a friend.

Cases of possession abound where a person or group has walked upon sacred ground, knowingly or unknowingly. Discarnates who are not Guardians may attach for the various reasons already discussed. Others can attach to teach someone a lesson about disrespect.

An Angry Warrior

An example of this kind of attachment was found involving a young female teenage client who went on a school camp-out into a forest area. No one knew that it was sacred ground to a tribe of Native Americans. The students were disrespectful and the trip taxed everyone's tolerance level. The leader of a group of discarnate warriors decided to teach one of the kids a lesson by attaching himself and his group to her. The trip was also plagued with bad weather.

During the inquiry, the warrior said that the girl spat on the land and that she was angry and abusive to the other kids in her group. It seems this pattern was part of her behavior prior to the trip, as we found other entities attached to her from before. The warriors were very willing to be released into the Light, after they told us of the situation and apology was given.

A Sacred Trail

The most common types of sacred ground here in Hawaii are the many ancient sacred trails. There are many stories of those who continue to see the "night marchers" who walk those physically unmarked pathways. They go from the mountains to the sea or from ancient village to village or to one of the many the sacred sites.

We were called to do a house clearing in Wailea, Maui. It was a vacation rental in the very high rent sector. No guest would stay a second night. They would vacate the next morning in a very frightened state. There was very strong activity in the house, including sounds, smell and touch, especially in the master bedroom.

As we called in the discarnates, a trail guard came forward, very upset. He complained about the existence of the house, but especially the bed in the master bedroom. Since the marchers only march at night and most embodied people sleep all night and the bed was sitting square on the trail, it created a problem.

Some of the marchers were even kicking the sleepers as they went over or around them!

I asked the trail guard if he had a solution as to what we could do to rectify the situation for all concerned. I told him that moving the house could not be done. The Hawaiian guard was silent for a moment. Meanwhile, I was consulting with our higher Guidance, that always comes through, even in the most bizarre circumstances. I asked the guard, with the greatest respect, if it would be possible to divert the trail just a little. I told him it would give total freedom for the marchers, as they would not be blocked by the embodied ones. I explained that things in his world were easily moved compared to the earthly task of moving something as large as a house! The guard was reluctant, but he agreed to the alteration giving one stipulation, "But we only agree to move the trail in "this" house, not any of the other eleven located elsewhere on the trail! And that the new trail must be marked so we can see it."

Roy, Suzanne and I looked at each other and telepathed, "WHAT?" I said to the guard, "Thank you for your generosity." Later we decided that if we were ever called to clear any of the eleven other houses, we would just cross that bridge, if and when we came to it.

The trail consists of astral energy and exists in the astral realm. We asked for Divine assistance in moving the trail. Suzanne, speaking as our crystal lady, remarked that we should use quartz pieces to "mark" the trail because crystals radiate energy, even into the astral. We had no quartz in our medicine bags (we do now), but we all had pennies which contain copper. Suzanne explained that higher frequency metals (gold, silver, copper, platinum, etc.) can work just as well, energetically speaking.

We all emptied our pockets and purses, even the agent representing the owner/client, and found enough penny markers. Suzanne crawled through the bushes with a flashlight (something we always do have), as it was night, and placed pennies all through the garden that runs along the side of the house and pool. We asked the guardian if the new path was satisfactory to them. He said it was and that they would use it.

We completed the clearing by releasing several other spirits. One was a foreign sailor from the whaling days who had been tied in a cave by the natives. He died of starvation in that cave and was very happy to be released. I wonder if he will have an aversion to Hawaii in his next life?

Closer Than You Think

Another "location," is being in a close relationship with someone who is already in attachment by discarnates.

Curses And Spells

It is our experience that another type of possession involves curses or spells. Curses are obviously placed with intent to do harm. Spells are sometimes cast for that purpose as well, but they can also be intended to help. Unfortunately, any kind of spell is manipulation when it is directed toward anyone else besides the one or more persons activating the spell, even if it is for "love." Manipulation goes against the free will choice of a person, even if you just want them to love you. Spells can often backfire or be countered with another spell. The fallout from this type of situation can have effects similar to a curse. For that reason, I will focus on curses.

A "curse maker" often enlists the assistance of negative spirits to weaken, scare, torment or even kill the intended prey. Some discarnates are literally slaves who have been captured by the practitioner who uses them. Others are actually sorcerers, wizards, witches or shamans of all types who cooperate with an embodied practitioner. They can manipulate those in body, with or without their awareness. In many cases there are organisms or creatures of various types, manipulated by the curse maker and attached to a victim with intention to impede them physically. Other sorcery "tools" are ritual manipulation of energy, telepathic mind manipulation, incantations (voice energy) and the use of potions, ceremonial objects or items belonging to the victim.

The most common myth about spells and curses is that one must believe in them to be influenced. This is not true—it is a myth. Many people are being influenced by curses that were placed on them and/or their families. There is another aspect to consider which is the ability of a given practitioner. Many curse-makers are very powerful and their work will be effective. Others are weak or lack knowledge of their craft and their work will have little or no effect on the intended victim(s).

Throughout history, there have been "practitioners of the Craft." The Craft is often referred to as Magic, and many past practitioners still reside in the astral. They are usually invisible and retain their skills and can expand their range by attaching to an embodied host. Hard to believe? Perhaps, but there are many accounts of their existence and many earthly laws dealing with those practices.

A curse can be imposed by the solicitor if they have the ability, or they can enlist a practitioner who is embodied or astral to do it for them, but always for a price. Some of these curses can last for generations and can be put upon a whole family. These situations still occur today all over the world. Each culture has their own unique form of "hocus pocus" and the practitioners to perform it. It is important for everyone to understand that the consulting with and manipulating of spirits of all varieties is still widely practiced all over the planet. These spells and curses can be released and we have dealt with a wide cultural assortment of them. I have included parts of transcripts of clearing sessions where we released curse energies and discarnates in the chapter on Exorcism.

In one situation where a curse was involved, our client told us he had gone to another practitioner before coming to us. A release process was done, by the first practitioner he went to, and the client was told that was all he could do for him. He told the client that if any of the curse remained and the client felt the need to find help again and another release was done…that it would go back to the three witches, who had cast the curse, and it would kill them!

This information was rather intense but we completed a release for him. We work within Divine Light energy and never intend harm to anyone, even dark witches…so, whatever the consequences may be from any clearing we do, are the karmic responsibility of those involved. The curse energy they had sent was very strong and we had been told, later, that two of the witches were ill and one had died. This is an example of one's own bad intention causing harm to the ones who sent it. This comes under the Law of Cause and Effect (what you put out will return to you).

Wizards, Witches And Witchcraft

I cannot possibly give a full coverage of this subject in this space but I do want to share some basic information. There are many books written on the vast topic of witchcraft covering information, historically and currently. Some of these are listed in the Bibliography. There have been numerous television programs focusing on this subject, with practitioners as guest speakers. I will focus on our encounters with witchcraft in the sessions of clearing and release for our clients. I would like to state here that we have met many witches who work in the Light and do not do any dark spells or curses. As with many things there are two paths to work with the same power. The choice is with the individual to work in the Light or the Dark.

There are many terms used for practitioners of the Craft: mystic, shaman, sorcerer, magician, medicine man/woman, wizard, witch, witch doctor, priest and the ultimate master, Magi. The most common term is witch, applied to both males and females. The term warlock is a misnomer. It is not the name for a male witch, rather, it is actually a traitor witch, and the term was used specifically during the Spanish Inquisition. A warlock would turn in another witch to be persecuted or worse.

The Inquisition was created for the purpose of eliminating all who were thought to be in competition with the Christian Church. This included all practitioners of the healing arts, whether private individual practitioners or covens (groups) of the Craft. They were declared pagans or devil-worshipers. Also included, were those who were simply suspect including homosexuals and the mentally retarded. All were persecuted. Over a period of about 300 years, it is estimated that 200,000 to 300,000 people were killed in Europe. Many were tortured before they died. Some are still in the astral plane.

The influence of the Christian Church/State political power-mongers extended over time throughout Europe where most all of whom practiced witchcraft were condemned to death by order of the Pope. That horrible action was fostered by The Church, The State and the newly emerging Medical Profession. They wanted complete control of the people and each of the respective healing services. The main focus for elimination was on the many female herbal practitioners present in every town and village. This attitude spread to America, where about 150 people were arrested, some tortured, and about 20 were killed in the Salem Witch Trials.

Eventually, the focus moved away from witchcraft to new science/medicine, a very limited replacement for natural science/spirit and the growing mechanism of urban industry. Many practitioners continued to practice in secret. As a result of those dark ages of propaganda and destruction, there are many people who still believe that all witchcraft involves satanic worship. Until recently, there were laws against any practice of the Craft, including the natural healing arts.

Here in Hawaii, in 1845, laws were written against any practices by Kahunas (priests/healers). This was done by religious and political leaders. It was part of their movement to bring Hawaii under American rule. Many local practitioners were quite busy at work, both Dark and Light, during those times because of the political issues of who would end up owning the Island Kingdom. Those laws were only lifted in 1968!!

The book titled, *The Donning International Encyclopedic Psychic Dictionary*, by June G. Bletzer, describes the term "Witch": "(Old English: wise person) 1. A seeker of knowledge; uses traditions, knowledge, psychic skills and rituals; dates back to the MAGI; one who is well versed in ASTROLOGY, astronomy, mind/ brain psychology, anatomy, PSYCHOMETRY, psychic sciences, AMULET ENERGIZING, POWER-OF-THE-WORD (voice [my insert]) and the laws of the ethereal world; 2. One who uses magic phenomena in one's religion; shows respect for the ethereal world DEITY who brings SUPERNATURAL power, and is capable of projecting psychical energy on another individual's SUBCON-SCIOUS MIND in order to manipulate the other; 3. One who can bend others to his or her will; 4. One who uses ceremonies and rituals in psychic work; hires him or herself out professionally for his or her psychic skills (both GOOD and EVIL); one who can give a BLESSING or a HEALING with success and work the PSYCHISM for the opposite and inflict a HEX…"

Many witches use herbal concoctions or alchemy, for healing or hurting someone. Some work alone and some work in groups or covens. The Craft is universal and can be found throughout recorded history. It is no different than any other craft or vocation, in that there are those who abuse the tools and skills and those who use them for good.

In the Hawaiian culture there is a form of witchcraft that creates a fireball that is sent to do harm to a person or location. The fire is very real and has created physical fires that have done real damage. Many years ago, my husband, Reuben, was a young deckhand sailing on a tugboat in the South Pacific on a late night watch. A crewmate was just coming up on deck to relieve him when they both saw a huge fireball coming out of the dark sky, directly toward Reuben. Simultaneously, Reuben shouted "ai kukae" while the crewmate (an older man) pushed him out of the way, shouting and waving-off the terrifying object. The fireball veered off and vanished in the night.

Reuben was quite shaken and was told by the crewmate to seek the help of a kahuna to find out who had sent it. Reuben did that when he returned home and was given the information and a release procedure.

In the same book, Bletzer describes the term "Witchcraft": "a craft of the wise; a religion paying homage to the one GOD; belief that man has fallen from the GODHEAD and will return to the Godhead by working to perfect himself; interested in what happens within themselves rather than what happens to their environment and lifestyle (Note: only those of dark practice, my insert); a revival of the magicians of the ancient past who had to disband during the Renaissance, while a few worked underground to save the knowledge; belief in the superiority of the mother goddess, who represents nature; emphasizes harmony with nature and tries to appeal to this harmony; uses ceremonies, rituals and amulets; belief in life after physical death and calls upon these intelligences along with the nature spirits for guidance, counsel, and protection; three distinct divisions: CLASSI-CAL WITCHES, GOTHIC WITCHES and NEOPAGAN WITCHES. (cf. WHITE MAGIC, ASSOCIATION MAGIC, CEREMONIAL MAGIC)."

Solicited Spirits

Occasionally, the relationship between the host and the discarnate is a voluntary attachment, with the host acting as the volunteer. This is the case with mediums, conscious channels, walk-ins, religious possession by the Holy Spirit, or various cultural deities. Speaking in "tongues," which is a totally foreign language, is done by certain western religious sects, such as the Pentacostals. Often, "faith healings" are part of these experiences.

In Latin America, many medical professionals utilize spiritual processes in the treatment of their patients, especially in cases of mental/emotional disorders, including multiple personality disorder, schizophrenia, epilepsy and delirium. These conditions are often the result of attachments "run amok." Those medical professionals acknowledge the reality of how discarnates can influence people in body. I encourage this type of understanding.

People have always called upon assistance from the spirit world. This includes "helpers." The most common spirit helpers are Angels. Most followers of western religion call upon the assistance of numerous types of Angels. We, as spiritual practitioners, could not be efficient without this assistance. Angels do not have physical bodies, so they are also in the category of discarnates but they are usually referred to as ethereal beings.

I must admit, I have been tempted to call upon deceased ancestors, who are still here with us, to do some damage control in certain situations. I have not done it, however, as it is a form of manipulation and there would be karmic con-sequences. We were asked to do a presentation on a T.V. show. The producer asked if we had any haunted house cases pending. I said no, but perhaps we could call a group into a house and create our own. We even had a friend who volun-teered their home. It was fun to think about for a brief moment—good for a laugh—but there would be no way to have any control. It was one of those "be careful what you ask for" situations. Again, unknown karmic consequences are not a wise choice. So, I mentioned we could do a clearing on the producer him-self...for the show...?

Elementals are also without physical bodies. They range from very low to very high intelligence—they are made of ethereal world elemental essence. They are actually members of the Angelic Kingdom. Many embodied people see and can communicate with them. Some elementals are friendly, some others are not. Folklore abounds throughout the world about these beings. Some familiar terms are fairies, gnomes, sylphs, leprechauns, elves and menehune (Hawaiian). In Scotland, the Findhorn community has developed an ongoing relationship with the elemental kingdom to assist in the farming of barren land with severe weather. Through this co-operative relationship with nature Spirits, they have produced incredible gardens and a very unique lifestyle.

Demon Helpers?

In the book, *Harper's Encyclopedia of Mystical & Paranormal Experience*, by Rosemary Ellen Guiley, she describes the meaning of the word "Demon." It means "replete with wisdom," as taken from the Greek DAIMON, meaning divine power, fate or god. The Greeks considered them to be intermediary spirits for deities or deified heroes in their communication with humans. Demons were like advisors of the gods. They could do good or evil through their advice or encounters with embodied humans. This is also true for embodied human helpers, is it not?

Guiley tells of Socrates, who spoke of his own demon guide who always helped him but never dictated. In Arabian lore a demon was called a DJINN. This is where the word Genie comes from. It is written that Solomon controlled his djinns with his magic ring. Then there is that story of the "gorilla!"

Unfortunately, the Catholic and other Christian churches seem to assume that all spirits are demons and that they are evil, to be cast out or destroyed. This is not possible, nor is destruction of any soul even appropriate!

Family Unity?

Many of the discarnates we release from our clients are family members. We often discover how family disharmony can continue to create dysfunction, long after death.

Our client, Maria, had been a Siamese twin (physically fused at the spine). The twins required surgery for survival, but only one lived. Maria's deceased twin attached to their mother at the time of her death, and remained even after their mother's death, many years later. Then, mother and sister attached to Maria. A few years later Maria came to us for a clearing.

Throughout Maria's youth, her relationship with her mother was very poor. Her mother was generally abusive to her. We began to inquire into the attitudes of the discarnate family members during the release process. We found that the sister had been angry and jealous for all those years because she had died while Maria lived. Those feelings were projected through the mother, to Maria. Later, after the mother died, mother attached to Maria. Then, with the sister attached to the mother who was now attached to Maria, the feelings seemed to come from within Maria herself. In reality, the feelings were coming from the discarnate family members in attachment.

After some extensive counseling with the deceased, who were still in great hostility, we released the sister and mother and peaceful balance was restored to Maria's life.

Release From A Distance

This case is another example of a family member in attachment. It is also one of many cases we process long distance, or absentee. In an absentee clearing, the client is not with us, for one reason or another. Perhaps they are in another town, state or country. It does not affect the process because we are dealing with the astral world where there is no time/space as we know it. We call the discarnates in through the vibration of a name or photo of the client or through a surrogate representing them.

One case we had involved a woman, Denise, whose mother died of cancer in a state of great resistance. Denise married several months later. Soon after her marriage, she began to exhibit very strange behavior. The condition worsened until her husband admitted her to a sanitarium. Denise's aunt (our client), Anita, went to visit her and felt that Denise was being manipulated by a discarnate. Anita confronted the entity and commanded it to leave. Denise struck out at her aunt and knocked her glasses off. Anita was not allowed to return to the sanitarium. She was told that she was too disruptive to the patient! She called me and we arranged a time to do an absentee release.

We prefer to work directly with the host, but there are situations where this is simply not possible. In these cases, we work with a loved one or close family member and the "spirit" of the host.

We asked Dona (of the group) to assist, as a "triad" is most powerful. Two of us were here on Maui, Anita was in another state, and Denise was in yet another state. We completed the release process over the phone. We discovered that the discarnate was, in fact, Denise's mother! She was very reluctant to let go, into the unknown, as she called it. We explained how harmful the attachment was for her daughter. Finally, she agreed to release if we would call upon Jesus to help her, and it was done.

A few days later, Anita was informed that Denise had "somehow" begun to recover from her "illness." To this day, her illness and complete recovery are unexplained by attending medical personnel.

On a psychic level, most of us would not refuse comfort to the spirit of a family member, but it really does not serve them or us to allow extended residence. They must be encouraged to complete earthly business and move into the Light.

Symptoms of Possession

Full possession is far more common than people realize and is rarely diagnosed. There are various symptoms, such as: chronic confusion, chronic depression or anxiety, nightmares, severe moodiness, memory loss, drug or alcohol abuse, sudden or unexplained deterioration of physical or mental health, etc. I believe that a very high percentage of cases that have been diagnosed as manic depression, schizophrenia, multiple personality disorder, bi-polar, and various forms of insanity…are, in fact, possession!

In the book, *Thirty Years Among the Dead*, Dr. Carl A Wickland describes numerous clearings he and his wife did on those who were in mental institutions. He states that most insanity cases involve possession. He also states that many acts of violence, crime and drug or alcohol abuse are situations with a high level of partial or complete possession.

Temporary Attachment

In this situation, a discarnate has attached to the aura of a person, attempting to get their attention for communication and/or to be released. This often happens to those who are psychically sensitive. There are many situations that can create this type of attachment. Some examples of this are: the host is passing a fatal car accident, the host is visiting a hospital or other location commonly inhabited by discarnates, a host/client on their way to a clearing, a host in the area of sudden or violent death of one or more people who can scatter as they leave their bodies, in the confusion of the event.

The attachment can manifest as sudden emotional change in the host, or simply feeling as though someone is there. If the discarnate cannot get a response from the host they will often go to someone else. Discarnates can also attach through a phone, from one host to another.

We have had the experience of a spirit who "jumped on" to a client as they were traveling to our appointment for release. They saw the Light and wanted to release. We have also had spirits just come in during a clearing and ask if they could go with the others who were being released into the Light—they happened to be in the neighborhood. In one instance, an entity begged, "Get me out of this bitch!"

Attraction

The first question usually asked by our client is, "Why?" Why does a discarnate attach to a specific person? This question is also one we always ask the discarnate entities attached to our clients. The entity always knows why and tells us. Once in a while, the host was just in a certain place at a certain time, available at some level.

Some people, especially children, are empathic in nature and literally take on the sorrow or pain of others. These people are usually very sensitive and can sense the suffering of a discarnate, and often see them. Childhood neglect and abuse creates a strong attraction for discarnates. Many of those spirits are children and some were killed by abuse and feel a kinship (like attracts like) to a host/child in a similar situation. Abused children often carry many spirits, as do adults who were abused as children. I go into this more in another chapter.

We had one case where a baby boy, under the age of two, was riding in a car that accidentally hit and killed a boy of four. The baby was an only child and lonely. He could see the young discarnate leave his body and beckoned to him to join him. They were together until the "baby" was in his late thirties and came to us for a clearing. The discarnate boy was very angry at the driver of the car, which happened to be the baby's mother. This created an undercurrent of dislike for the mother by the "baby" (client), which continued up to the time of the clearing. Those feelings were coming through her son, from the discarnate boy/victim who was in attachment for all those years.

Attraction often occurs when people open themselves, unknowingly, by using alcohol or drugs. Abuse of these substances creates holes in the aura and distorts emotions. An extreme example of this is a client of ours who took a substance called "Syrian root" to seek knowledge about his spiritual path, also called a vision quest. He had a five-year history of regularly ingesting a synthetic drug called "ecstasy." He went to a remote beach for this journey. The effects of this experiment literally blew a large hole in his auric field on the left side of his head.

Astrals were pouring into that hole. It was incredible! He was seeing them constantly, in front of his car, in the rearview mirror, everywhere. When this happens, you can forget about sleeping...you are like a traveling circus. When he came to us his health had rapidly deteriorated, along with his sanity. After his clearing, he required some auric repair to seal the holes or tears in the aura. This repair can be done by those who do magnetic healing—or other type of auric energy balance of the body. In a case like this it is also suggested to create a good nutritional program to re-build the body.

Negative emotional patterns are the weakest link in our general health and also the strongest attraction for discarnates with similar patterns. The astral realm is full of deceased people, who all have one or more dysfunctional emotional conditions...that is why they are stuck there.

The Dead Are Upon You

There are numerous health conditions of the body, mind and spirit that can attract discarnates. Many practitioners in health care are susceptible to discarnate attachment, due to the nature of their work. Here is a list of specific health conditions or situations most associated with discarnate attachment or full possession:

1. Alternative health practitioners who touch or counsel their clients

2. All personnel employed in medicine or police work

3. Those who enter war zones, prisons, bars, graveyards, morgues, hospitals, sanitariums

4. Those with chronic poor health, anyone having surgery, transplant recipients

5. Those with chronic depression, postpartum depression, negative attitudes, epilepsy, autism or a violent nature, abuse victims

6. Those with schizophrenia, multiple personality disorder, Tourette Syndrome

7. Those with chronic criminal behavior, ghoulish fascinations, insanity

8. Those bound up in fanaticism of any kind, including religious

9. All UFO abductees

10. Those with suicidal tendencies, nightmares

11. Alcoholics, drug addicts and other substance abusers

12. Anyone who lives with someone who fits into one or more of these categories.

Let us pause here, take a deep breath, and relax. I do not want to instill fear with this information—hopefully it is assisting you. If it is strongly disturbing to you, it could be that you have a resident "guest" making you feel uncomfortable!

If you think that you, or someone you know, have one or more guests, don't become alarmed. It is best to stay calm. If you want to know if there is an attachment, you can ask in meditation or consult a practitioner who specifically works in this field. Try to find one who has been referred to you because of their proficiency.

If you are concerned about your own susceptibility to possession, be honest with yourself regarding your emotional and physical condition. This would be a good time to avail yourself of the Ho'oponopono, a personal cleansing. Then use the Cleansing and Blessing Ceremony to clear your premises. You can also utilize the protection of The Blue Egg. Call upon Archangel Michael and your Spirit Guides to assist you (refer to the Toolbox chapter).

Assistance

Those of us who do this work are tapped on the auric shoulder often. We have given permission to be of service to those discarnates seeking release. This is not possession or attachment, but being available for assistance. The important thing is to assist these soul/spirits into the Light, not into your self. These beings are PEOPLE—lost souls, and should be treated with consideration and respect!

There are practitioners who refer to spirits as spooks, boogies, garbage, parasites, the unclean or demons. They attempt to dispose of these souls by casting them into a bottomless pit, a body of water, hell, the sun, up some cosmic vacuum cleaner or many other (inappropriate) disposal locations. These practices come out of ignorance, fear and judgement…I suggest that some of these spirits are our own family members or loved ones. I also suggest that a negative karmic load could be created by this type of practice.

I encourage all practitioners to do expansive clearings at this time but please do them with awareness, compassion and integrity. The planet Earth is in great need of cleansing of all contrary thought forms from the embodied and discarnate. These negative thought forms are a powerful contamination of our atmosphere.

The releasing of spirits and contrary energies usually requires a living person in a physical body to be the catalyst. This is due to the power we have in our connection to the Earth, a powerful living organism which sustains us, and our connection to cosmic energies from which we receive our Light. I was once criticized with the statement: "You spend more time in other dimensions than you do in this one." Yes, perhaps I do, but that is where the work has led me. I have met some wonderful people there and have had the privilege of sharing very special moments with them. They too, are our clients. These experiences have expanded my awareness and enhanced my ability to deal with the traumas of the physical world.

Specific Symptoms & Conditions

In the following section, I will be describing other types of attachment with specific symptoms and/or resulting conditions that are unique. Some of these symptoms or conditions have been given medical labels.

Postpartum Depression

This condition seems to have a very broad spectrum of symptoms. At the low end, there is mild depression (baby blues). I feel this can be easily explained by hormonal fluctuation, sleep deprivation, psychological re-adjustment, or side effects of the drugs given to the mother.

At the far end of the spectrum, some mothers have thoughts and feelings of violence, even toward their children (psychosis). Wanting to murder one's own child goes quite far beyond the common medical diagnosis of chemical imbalance due to hormonal fluctuation. I feel that in reality, these are two separate conditions, with different causes.

Some of these mothers, particularly those dealing with the more severe feelings, display classic symptoms of possession: mood swings, severe depression, suicidal thoughts, homicidal thoughts or unexplained violent behavior.

There is a high probability that most of these women delivered their babies in hospitals, a common location for discarnates. Is it possible that these mothers are taking home more than their new babies? I suggest that inquiry be made to address the possibility of attachment or worse.

Organ Transplants

Receiving a transplanted organ can also create a situation of discarnate attachment with numerous symptoms that create stress for the host, because the owner of the organ is still attached! This is an example of "medicine" ignoring spirit, as it EXPERIMENTS with nature. Nature is already perfect and each person chooses the imperfections of their own body for very good reasons having to do with their need to experience those imperfections in a given lifetime. It is always a karmatic choice made at a soul level prior to coming into a given lifetime.

One aspect of that choice is to educate oneself about good health, to become aware of one's body and its functions and to choose a natural, healthy lifestyle. That decission can lead to a path of preventative maintenance and natural healing procedures. Never the less, the organ transplant surgeries are increasing as "technology" expands. These patients and their doctors need to acquire an understanding of Spirit to see the whole picture as it applies to the situation of transplanting the organ of one person into the body of another.

The original owner of an organ stays with an organ that has been kept viable, because it is still ALIVE! The soul/spirit does not normally vacate their body until ALL of it is dead. The blueprint of the DNA and the cellular memory of the original owner are contained within each organ. Every cell, all life, has memory of its experience. A given organ has the same memory as the rest of the body it was living in. And that is just something the recipient takes on—the good, the bad and the ugly.

There was a television program about organ recipients and their "new experiences" and the many similarities they all had in common. Some of those experiences include having dreams about strangers, drastic changes in emotional patterns, various habits, food preferences and personality traits. These symptoms were found to be shared with the families of deceased donors, and verified to be those traits and habits of their departed loved ones. I would suggest a psychic inquiry or hypnosis regression for any recipient, to identify any "visitors," and a subsequent spirit release and/or soul fragment retrieval to clear the situation.

There have also been cases where a newly attached discarnate has created great friction or even separation between the host and their partner or mate. Unhappy spirits can cause great disturbance in the earthly relationships of the host.

The same situation applies to blood transfusions, although to a lesser degree. One does experience effects from carrying another person's DNA in their body and perhaps takes on an essence of the blood donor's soul energy. Over time it will dissolve as the blood merges with your own. The amount of blood taken in is also a factor. Again, it is a matter of degree. It is a good idea to inquire about the possible influence of the donor. At the very least, proceed with a Ho'ponopono process between yourself and the donor(s). You don't need to know who or how many—simply state "all" during your process.

Many people now give blood before their own surgery, or just to keep it in storage for possible need in the future. If that can't or hasn't been done is always best to receive blood from one's own family, if possible.

Pathogenic Micro-organisms

These are organisms that cause infection. There are many different varieties but the main catagories of species are: Virus—Bacteria—Fungus. They are all intelligent "beings" but they are just very, very little and can't be seen by the human eye without the aid of a microscope. Most of us carry colonies of these beings in our bodies naturally. The point at which they become a threat to our health is when they increase their population inside of us to a point where it compromises our immune system. This is commonly referred to as an infection.

The infection can be systemic (involving the major systems throughout the body) or it can be specific (involving only one organ or limited area in the body). Either way, an infection, which is left untreated, can worsen and/or spread. All infection is potentially dangerous.

I have included these "beings" in this list because they too are entities in attachment. The process of "clearing" these types out of the body, is similar to the one we use for discarnate humanoids. I also suggest the use of natural remedies to aid the body in healing from the effects of the organisms and to choose a process to release the negative emotional patterns that begin the weakening process in the body (as described in books by Louise Hay, (see bibliography). Prevention through balancing the needs of the Body, Mind and Spirit is the ideal course toward good health.

Issues of Sexuality

There are many people who are tormented by feelings they don't understand or can't control in regard to their gender or sexual desires. The general categories of these issues I am speaking of are: Transvestites, Transsexuals, Bisexuals, Homosexuals, Celibates, Nymphomaniacs and men with Excessive male sexual appetite. I am not addressing those of these categories or combinations of, who are comfortable with their preferences. I am speaking of those who are not comfortable with their feelings and those in confusion about what they are feeling.

May I suggest that an inquiry be done to see if there is possible discarnate attachment. If a person is in self rejection of their desires or behavior, they can ascertain if their desires are truly their own or someone else's. At least they would be able to make a very personal choice from a perspective of sovereignty. We have had numerous cases where one or more discarnates were acting out their desires through the host who was simply overpowered by the energy.

This is not, in any way, a condemnation, or a judgement of any person or their sexuality.

Body Dismorphic Disorder

There is very little known about this disorder but a doctor who treats these patients wrote a book about it in 1996. "The Broken Mirror" is about, "Understanding and treating Body Dysmorphic Disorder," by Katherine A. Phillips, M.D. People with this condition are preoccupied or even obsessed with how some part of their physical appearance looks. To them, some aspect of their body is repulsive, hideous or abhorrent. For some, the obsession forces them to continually seek a reflective surface (mirrors, windows, etc.) to keep looking, in disbelief and hoping it will suddenly vanish. The most unusual part of these cases is that no one else can "see" the defect!

Dr. Phillips writes, "They've thought that their face is too wide, their stomach is too fat, or their eyes look ugly. Or that their facial muscles are sagging, their skin has marks or scars, their penis is too small, that…Some have surgery after surgery without ever being satisfied with how they look. Many haven't told a single soul…They feel too embarrassed and ashamed." For others who do tell someone, they have to deal with the reaction. "and the people they tell can't see the "defects" or consider them to be minimal, they feel miserable, isolated and misunderstood."

I suggest discarnate attachment could be a key to many of these cases. If you can imagine seeing an overlay of someone else's face in your mirror, every time you look, perhaps you can relate to this traumatic condition. And because this disorder can be so devastating to the lives of those afflicted, I encourage an inquiry be done, through hypnosis, to establish the possible influence of discarnate spirits.

Bulimia—Anorexia

These two conditions are both considered to eating disorders and they are often present in combination in the same patient. I would like to simply add them to this list because they fit into the symptomology category of possible entity attachment or possession. The behavior is uncontrollable and unexplainable. Even with extensive professional medical care, patterns of abnormal eating continue. I suggest an inquiry be done with these cases, especially because the disorder(s) often causes death.

Schizophrenia

I wish to include the phenomena of Schizophrenia because I believe it is related to possession. It is described as a form of psychosis in which a patient dissociates from their environment and deteriorates in character and personality—sometimes displaying bizarre or delusional behavior. It is often called "split personality." The most common symptom is hearing voices. This is a major symptom of the presence of discarnates in strong attachment. Unfortunately, the medical profession states that, "there is no cure." Medication is usually given to depress the symptomology. These people are often placed in a sanitarium—remember the niece?

It is my feeling that many, if not the majority of these cases are due to severe or full possession. I believe they could be cleared of this condition with an inquiry and then a process to release the entities in possession. Hypnosis can be a valuable tool, especially for the purpose of discovering attached discarnates. This should be done by a practitioner who is familiar with this type of inquiry work, and who is emotionally stable themselves. Discarnates can be very nasty and manipulative.

A client was referred to us to release an entity who came through her at random. As we began the clearing session, the client, a woman of seventy years of age, began to speak rapidly in an African language. The tone was that of someone who was alarmed! We discovered it was a deceased African witchdoctor who was chastizing everyone present and angry that we were disturbing him.

He had attached to her from childhood, where she was raised, in South Africa. He became outwardly vocal and disturbed as she became elderly and experienced a time of crisis in her life. He was very angry and wanted to choke me to death to stop the session. Fortunately, we always have Angelic help with these entities, even though one of our group told us afterward that she sat on her hands because he was trying to get her to reach over and do the strangling for him. In the meantime, we completed the clearing.

Multiple Personalities

Another, more incredible and less common condition is that of Multiple Personality Disorder (MPD). These are people displaying three or more distinctly different "personalities." Most have ten to thirteen, some have as many as one hundred, that appear off and on. Many people with this affliction can be found in sanitariums and prisons. A common thread that runs through almost all of these cases is that the person was traumatized by sexual molestation as a child.

I offer four possible explanations for these cases:

1. During trauma, the conscious mind implodes and withdraws from control because it can't control the situation, or stop it. At this time, the subconscious draws from past-life aspects of the self to continue to function. Since we experience a variety of personages, culture and both genders in various incarnations, this accounts for the variety in the new personalities.

2. During trauma, the conscious mind implodes and withdraws, leaving the person wide open to the many spirits waiting for a host.

3. Psychological or biological dysfunction caused by other factors.

4. A combination of any of the above.

I believe that number 2 is the strongest probability with some or all of the other factors involved to a lesser degree. In any case, I recommend an inquiry into the history of the person to establish the situation at onset and cause. Regressive hypnosis or other similar practice would facilitate this process.

Common possession (attachment) may also involve more than one discarnate, but it is not as obvious because the original core personality does not leave, the discarnates only filter through it. The behavior of MPD's is usually more radical because the discarnates often take over total control of the host and exhibit a dramatic range of personality and behavioral expressions. Each individual entity is manifesting as him/herself, just as differently as any three people in physical bodies. There is far less "filtering" going on due to the level of control utilized by the deceased residents.

One of the most well documented cases of multiple personalities was that of Billy Milligan (twenty four different personalities). His story is told in the book, *The Minds of Billy Milligan*, by Daniel Keyes. I would like to present an outline of the story of Billy, changing only one word. I am replacing the word "personality" with the word "discarnate," as that is how I view the case.

Billy was sickly the first year of his life, and was in and out of the hospital. He had several imaginary playmates (discarnates?) at a very early age. His father committed suicide after years of alcoholism, and Billy's mother remarried. When Billy was nine, his stepfather began brutally sodomizing him. More entities were attracted to Billy as he suffered with his emotional and physical pain. They began moving in and out of "the spotlight" (control) with increasing frequency. The sexual abuse continued until Billy moved away from home at age seventeen.

Billy had attempted suicide at sixteen by jumping from the school roof. One of the entities stopped him (to keep their energy source alive?) and the personality of Billy withdrew. The whole group of attached entities kept him asleep, if you will, because they knew he would try suicide again. They moved in and out of the spotlight, performing various functions, rather like a team. Some spoke different languages. There were males and females of different ages, cultural backgrounds, and with different talents or abilities. A few were children, the rest were adults. Some were right handed, some left. Some wore glasses, others didn't. Billy's body demonstrated various characteristics, talents, skills, speech/language, gender traits, activities and health conditions as each discarnate would take the spotlight. They all responded to the name Billy, to hide their own identity, but the host personality remained asleep for six years. He spent years in and out of trouble as the various discarnates demonstrated their different frustrations and desires.

Then came the crimes that led to his incarceration. One male discarnate would pick up a woman to rob her, but while they were together a lesbian discarnate would move into the spotlight to seduce her, out of a desire for affection. Billy was tried on three rape charges, moved in and out of various psychiatric hospitals, and was permanently incarcerated at Athens Mental Health Center, in 1982.

I feel that Billy was dealing with entity attachment prior to age nine, due to his hospitalizations and sorrowful childhood. When the sexual trauma overwhelmed him, more entities moved in. After the suicide attempt, Billy thought he was dead. The discarnates totally took over (full possession) and increased in number—the more vacancy, the more room available!

Psychiatric professionals attempt to merge what they perceive as one personality that has fragmented. Their goal is to create a "new and improved" personality.

I would propose releasing the discarnates (excess personalities)—then retrieving the one personality (core/host) through regressive hypnosis, connect to the "inner child" aspect to heal the causative trauma.

The incredible changes that occur when an "alter personality" (discarnate) takes the spotlight, are because another separate soul/spirit is literally manifesting through the body/mind of the host, who has all but moved out of his/her body! This explains all the manifestation of the differences between the various personalities. Some examples of these are: behavior indicative of the opposite sex (than that of the host), different brain wave patterns, health conditions, language spoken, different ages and completely different identities with histories that are unrelated to the "core personality" (owner of the body). Some are left-handed, some are right, some require glasses, others don't, some have a physical impairment (such as a limp), some have specific skills the host does not have and finally but most obvious, they each have their own name, don't we all? All you have to do is ask them!

Each soul/spirit (person) carries their own vibration or blueprint, even beyond death. The physical body is only a shell for that vibration to manifest through. One or more blueprints, such as those of discarnates, can strongly manifest through another (overlay]) even more so when the host all but vacates it's body—as in multiple personality cases. The unconscious mind is very open and susceptible to all outside influences, especially when the conscious mind is asleep or being traumatized with the terror, pain and disbelief caused by an abhorrent experience.

In his book, *People of the Lie*, Dr. M. Scott Peck describes cases of Multiple Personality Disorder (MPD) that were actually those of possession. Patients were healed when exorcism was done. Dr. Ralph Allison, psychiatrist, wrote of MPD cases in his book, *Minds in Many Pieces*. He also cites cases that were directly caused by possession involving one or more discarnates.

I would like to point out the danger of ignoring the reality that many, if not most, MPD cases are caused by full possession. I drop to my knees to plead, beg and implore those in medical practice and the clergy to awaken and explore the Spirit in all things. Do it in private if you fear ridicule. First decide if you are a healing assistant or a mechanic. I honor the courage of those of you who already have made that decision.

Aka Cords

There is a unique type of attachment called "psychic cording." Within the Huna practices it is referred to as an "aka" cord. These are actual strings of etheric substance hooked into one or more chakra points (energy centers) of the body. The main points for attachment on the body are located at: the belly under the navel, the center stomach, the heart, the throat and the third eye (between the brows). They can be as thin as spaghetti, or the size of a small tree trunk! Negative feelings, conscious or unconscious, can create these undesirable connections to or from another person. Usually, the other person is in a physical body. If the other person is a discarnate, it is usually a relative or loved one.

ALL aka cord attachments are undesirable. They emanate to and from people through weaknesses in their auric field caused by negative feelings; insecurity, worry, fear, jealousy, anger, revenge, etc. These attachments are an energy drain for the one BEING corded and energy food for those DOING the cording.

Most people attach cords from a sub-conscious level and are unaware of doing it. There are those, however, who do it consciously for the purpose of manipulation of thoughts or feelings. This can also be done in the casting of spells and curses.

If you have aka cords, you may feel various sensations in the body at the point of connection. These have been described as: nausea, pain, twisting, pulling, tightness, or just a general lack of energy. If you ever had the feeling of being "torqued" at the thought of a particular person, there are probably one or more aka cords between the two of you. Emotions travel through these cords, often creating a severe emotional reaction to a person or situation. You can have several cords from several people at the same time. You can have cords attached with loved ones as well as enemies.

Another source of aka cord attachment can be from a speaker or performer addressing an audience, whether in person or through televised broadcast! Television evangelists, entertainers and sports figures fall into this category. The effects of T.V. and radio on the audience create altered states of consciousness creating an "open channel" in the viewer/listener. There can be influences from subliminal programming, astral entities or aka cord attachment. Casino gambling is another arena for this activity due to the strong negative emotions of greed, fear, guilt or anger often found in the patrons.

The most important thing you can do for yourself or a relationship is to remove the aka cords. This will assist you in dealing with that person/source from a clear perspective, releasing the emotional entanglements. Love between people creates a merging at a spirit/soul level, so the removal of aka cords does not sever this aspect of a relationship in any way. In fact, it opens the opportunity to improve the quality of that love by raising the vibrations as you release the lower vibrational attachments. We use this process extensively in our clearing work. The process for removing aka cords is described in the Toolbox chapter.

Soul Retrieval

There is another situation we encounter in our work, which is called soul fragmentation. To correct this condition by retrieving various fragments and drawing them back to the core essence we do a process called "Soul Retrieval." Let us first look at what the soul is. Many descriptions have been given and I will try to simplify the subject.

The SOUL is consciousness, intelligence—the SPIRIT is the energy for it, the energy of the universe. Together, they are life expressing itself. All things, animate or inanimate, have intelligence. It has been stated that there is only ONE soul, ultimately. Thus, we are all one…totality expressing itself individually through the catalyst of spirit…in, on, around and through self and each other.

Soul/Mind is the subconscious, conscious and superconscious in all things, and it has memory of its total experience of immortal existence. People have or are soul/spirit whether they are embodied or not. Now that I have shared the basics, I will address "soul loss."

What does soul loss look like? What are the symptoms? The conditions of dissociation or coma can reflect severe soul loss. Milder conditions reflect the same symptomology as attachment or possession, which are: chronic confusion, depression, nightmares, memory loss or general deterioration of physical or mental health, to name a few.

The term "loss" can be deceptive, as it implies that the soul is gone, but it has memory via mind, so it can be located. Complete soul loss is rare. I feel this is a possible condition in the instance of zombies. Most who write on the subject of zombies list all the poisons that are used to create the condition, and that the use of them is standard procedure. They also agree that complete soul detachment or enslavement (by the practitioner) is a very high probability. I agree, in theory, however, we have never had occasion to work with a zombie.

There are more common situations of soul loss or "Fragmentation." Often, a portion of the soul/mind stays with a body upon physical death, especially if the death was sudden, violent or otherwise traumatic. Fragmentation can occur in the situation of a past life death where a soul/mind fragment remains with the body and/or the location. In the meantime, another portion of "that" same soul reincarnates and is embodied today and still in contact with any soul/mind fragments at a distance.

A soul fragment can also be sold or given for some type of exchange. Perhaps that is where the term, "I would sell my soul for…" comes from. A soul portion can also be rejected or left in a place for safety, from a subconscious level, during a situation of terror. Hypnosis and/or communication with one's inner child (kino aka) can be very helpful in these types of retrievals. The child can "take" you to the past situation and regressive hypnosis can be the vehicle for that process. At that point I activate Ho'oponopono, which is the catalyst for release.

Think of the soul as a "mother clump" of dough to make sourdough bread. Once that is created, it can be maintained in dough form indefinitely, with careful feeding and watering. From that mother clump numerous loaves of bread can be made, year after year. Imagine each of those loaves representing a different lifetime for that soul. And just as one can make two or more loaves of bread at the same time, from the same clump—we can also exist in two or more lifetimes (as one or more different species) simultaneously. To take it one step farther, small pieces (fragments) can be taken from each loaf of bread. Each piece is identical in substance to the loaf and to the clump.

Soul retrieval is often part of our work when clearing a discarnate attachment, depending on who or what is attached. It is very common with curses. After completion of Ho'oponopono for the client, we call upon angelic assistance to seek out and escort any soul fragments that may be contained in some way and then we assist the client to "call in" all fragments, back unto him or her self. The owner is the only one who can do that, the only one with the "authority," if you will.

Soul fragments can be located and reclaimed. This often requires the assistance of a practitioner. The memory (within the soul/mind) that is associated with the occurrence of the fragmentation is also retrieved, so there may need to be some follow-up counseling to process possible trauma from the recalling/re-assimilation of that memory.

Soul retrieval is a common practice by indigenous shamans all over the world. Shamanism acknowledges the soul/spirit in all things and the need for harmony between all beings, including flora and fauna and the elements of earth itself. It teaches that disharmony causes disease and dysfunction to the whole.

An interesting story was told to me by a Viet Nam War veteran. To prevent being lost in the jungle and to be able to return to an exact spot that could not be marked with anything physical, because of possible enemy discovery, he stated that he left a piece of his "mind" as a marker. He had no trouble finding the location later. This is an example of intentionally leaving a soul fragment, which was retrieved. This could come in very handy, especially for children! I suggest education to expand one's awareness. Some suggested reading is listed in the Bibliography by authors, Sandra Ingerman, Joseph Campbell, and others.

Ignorance Can Be Dangerous

Some spirits enjoy the activities available through the physical host. Others literally attempt to destroy their host because of their own emotional dysfunction. There are cases where the host does not want to release the entities. The host relies on them to give help with knowledge/information, physical ability, protection or emotional support. In some cases, the host is lonely and the spirits provide companionship. These people/hosts do not realize the true nature of their condition, nor do medical personnel who may be treating them.

Anyone who claims to be a walk-in and everyone who does trance channeling, are likely hosts for attachment or full possession. These cases can often occur be through mutual agreement, depending on the awareness of the host, regarding matters of Spirit. I believe that as much as 80% of our population is dealing with attachment/possession, and that ALL of us, at one time or another, have or will have some type of contact with these issues.

I encourage metaphysical education, so there can be understanding of the very nature of Spirit and Universal Law which prevails—belief is not required, it happens anyway! Possession interferes with the conscious free will of both parties. Careful COMMUNICATION and UNDERSTANDING are the keys to releasing lost souls, replacing soul parts and shedding Light upon the entire issue of the non-physical worlds.

Many of the greatest minds and teachers in history acknowledge the reality of the spirit world and the influence discarnates have upon those in a physical body. All indigenous cultures and their Sacred writings/teachings confirm this as well. I look forward to the time when those of the collective medical profession expand their minds beyond the physical reality, so they can realize the true nature of humankind and how it relates to our health. I also look forward to the time when our clergy are re-educated about the true nature of our spirituality and how it relates to our lives…and deaths!

A refusal to acknowledge the spirit world is beyond caution—it is dangerous! Unfortunately, the reality of attachment/possession is not accepted by most medical practitioners, and few clergy are educated about its true nature. This closes off the two main avenues for the general education of the public and the services that could be given to assist those dealing with discarnate spirits in their lives.

All of the astral plane (and all other planes) are included in the entire awakening process that we are experiencing at this time in our evolution. They cannot be dormant, all life is in constant motion of contraction/expansion. Those in the astral are being activated and enlightened by the same cosmic energies as we are, to expand their experience and awareness of the reality of their existence, and evolve. It is time to move out of ignorance and judgement and fear, and the suffering that it causes. It is time to move into awareness and re-education about "the dead." Physical death is a journey every one of us will be taking...again!

Extraterrestrials

"Extraterrestrial" refers to beings whose origin is not the planet Earth. I wish to make a brief statement about this subject, simply to acknowledge the reality of the interaction that I do believe is taking place between earthlings and E.T.'s.

We have encountered these beings through working with "contactees" during hypnosis and clearing sessions, where E.T.'s were monitoring and/or manipulating the lives of humans. The tools and processes we use for attachment/possession are the same as those we use for contactees. It is the same situation, with very different entities in attachment (many are discarnate but they are not dead). I will not go into any description of those sessions in this book, perhaps in the next one.

Awareness

The subject of E.T.'s evokes mixed reactions from people. Some think it is hogwash and others react with fear or fascination. Many of the books, films and documents from all cultures tell of earthly visitations throughout history. There are extensive and detailed accounts of the encounters of recent abductees. I encourage everyone to be open to the reality that we live in a limited third-dimensional classroom, which provides for the many lessons that are to be learned in a physical existence—but we also exist in a multi-world, multi-dimensional, multi-time/space continuum, filled with other inhabitants. It is important that people become aware of other-worldly beings. Even though they are usually unseen, many are interacting with our world and some are very much a part of it. This interaction has been going on since the beginning of life on Earth.

Who Are They?

There are many different sources of information on the various species of E. T.'s throughout history, from ancient Sumerian records, Hindu illustrations and writings, to current reports of pleasant and unpleasant personal experiences. There is also much channeled material. Discernment is the key. The scenarios regarding who the E.T.'s are and what they are doing here are too numerous to go into—there is much misinformation and disinformation involved. My experience is that there is far more human interaction with E.T's than most people realize.

Often, there is very little memory of an encounter until triggered by a book, movie, dream or other catalyst. This triggering often leads a person to utilize hypnosis to discover information of the experience. These experiences range from terror to ecstasy. There are accounts of scary E.T's and those who have saved, helped or given spiritual guidance to earthlings. As with all things, there seem to be the "bad guys" and the "good guys," but the good guys never abduct anyone against their will, they invite.

Abductees state that although the aliens appear to have physical bodies, they are able to levitate and move through walls and other objects. They utilize energy to control or immobilize people, and to communicate telepathically. Contactees have reported that they have been rendered helpless under these influences. Cases have been reported where abduction was avoided when a strong statement of refusal was made. These statements consisted of firm spiritual conviction and intent. For example: "I command you to leave in the name of Christ—I do not give my permission to you for any reason whatsoever!" One could use the terms God, Jesus, Divine Creator, Christ Light or any other similar term of your preference. The important ingredient is your BELIEF in what you say. If you feel you are involved in this type of encounter, you can say no.

On a spiritual level, everything that is happening is like a test for all of us, as we need to make some important choices in our lives. These choices have to do with our survival on a physical level, as well as our condition on a soul/spirit level.

Will we accept guidance from beings who are trying to assist in our spiritual growth? Or, will we submit in fear to malevolent beings whose only interest is their own agenda? AND, how do we tell the difference between them? It is time to re-evaluate our priorities in life, recognize our own divine nature and realize that Divinity comes from within, not without.

Whether we are dealing with E.T.'s or our next-door neighbors, we must LEARN to discern the Dark from the Light, Fiction from Truth. We must stop fearing the one and deifying the other. We must take responsibility for our own choices and make them from an educated perspective. We must learn to integrate the dark and the light, the contrary and the harmonious. To fear the dark, is to give it power, and create imbalance. To shine light upon it, is to give it understanding, and create harmony.

Beam Me Up Scotty...

For those of you who are fascinated with the whole idea of extraterrestrials and space travel, I encourage you to continue that fascination—it is part of our heritage and certainly, our future. But there are many who believe that benevolent E.T.'s are going to beam the good people (the chosen) off the planet for their salvation. We all need to understand that we must master this earthly existence in balance and harmony before ever being allowed to proceed into space or even beyond the physical cycles of incarnation. No one outside yourself will save you. You are the only one qualified to do it. The answers are within YOU...

During an individual clearing session we encountered two earth humans who were not deceased and they were not on this planet! They had signed contracts to work at a "location" out in space, away from this world. They were part of a secret (obviously) project. Unfortunately, they were contracted for a mandatory time of two years. They did not want to be there any longer, even though they had not been there very long. There seemed to be no way out. They had decided to meditate together and do a process we call "mind projection" or "remote viewing", to find some kind of help outside of their location. With either of those procedures, there is no limit to distance one can go. They were searching the earth plane because it was their home and they connected to our vibration, which was strong during the session—like a neon sign in the ethereal world.

The sad fact was that we could not release them—they were not dead. I told them we could make a plea for them, for Angelic assistance or other appropriate beings, who may have jurisdiction. This was a "first" for us (there are many in our work) and that is when we utilize our creative imagination and the highest spiritual authority available. The advice was for them to request Divine assistance from their own heavenly "team" to help them leave the project as soon as possible. Within our authority, we were able to request Divine intervention to give them freedom and protection in their quest.

Long ago, the father of a friend of mine, David (who was born clairvoyant) gave him some wonderful advice. I wish to share it with you. His father said, "take care not to become so spaced out, that you are no earthly good!"

Exorcism

The Hawaiian word for exorcism is "wehe" (vay-hay). The translation is: To open, untie, undo, loosen, undress, uncover, unfasten, unlock, unwrap, exorcise, unhook, cleanse of defilement, remove, forgive, to satisfy. This is the translation from the Hawaiian Dictionary, written by Mary Kawena Pukui and Samuel H. Elbert.

In the English-speaking world the meanings are different. The word "exorcism" means: "Greek: exousia, oath—Lat./Eng.: adjure, put the spirit on oath or evoking a higher authority to compel the entity to act in a way contrary to it's wishes. Such compulsion also implies binding." This is an explanation from two books, one titled, *Harper's Encyclopedia of Mystical & Paranormal Experience* and the other titled, *The Encyclopedia of Ghosts and Spirits*, both by Rosemary Ellen Guiley (see Bibliography). I have used both of these books as references for some of the information in this chapter.

Another explanation of the word exorcism is found in, *The Donning International Encyclopedic Psychic Dictionary*, by June G. Bletzer. It states that exorcism is defined as: "to remove evil forces or negative influences from a person or area, using a special technique or ritual..."

In The World Book Dictionary, the word exorcise is defined as: "1. To drive out (an evil spirit) by prayers, ceremonies or the like..." 2. To free (a person or place) from an evil spirit; to purify..."

The Hawaiian translation denotes a process of kindness, compassion and healing. All the English explanations put a very negative stigma on the process of exorcism. Many of the rituals around the world, past and present, are based in fear and are harsh because of the negative attitudes about the world towards the dead. Some intense exorcisms involve physical pain, flying objects, convulsions, swearing and literally, battle between the discarnate and the practitioner. This can take a very severe toll on the practitioners' life force energy, at the very least.

Some intense processes include the use of loud incantations, threatening prayers, beating the victim or shock treatment—then the burning of offensive incense, herbs or other concoctions—all this after purging the victim physically, from each end of their body, or cutting off all their hair. And then, another favorite of the past was the "burning at the stake."

In his book, Exorcism, Eugene Maurey describes a bizarre method of exorcism done by the "Puritans" in 17th century America. The process involved a teeter-totter board with a chair at one end. The "victim" was tied to the chair while men at the other end lowered the poor soul into the water. If the person survived this process, they were declared free of the evil influence of demonic possession.

Electricity applied to the base of the spine was also a form of exorcism, a dreadful experience. Electro shock therapy is being used today to deal with such cases as schizophrenia (which I believe are situations of possession) and other severe personality disorders (ditto). Electric shock can release a discarnate, but not always. This is a dangerous practice on any part of the body, under any circumstances, and should be acknowledged as destructive and eliminated as a therapeutic method of any kind. The medical people have no awareness of the effect this has on the general condition of the body, mind and spirit of the patient.

Please, dear God! This is not necessary. There is another way. If one just antagonizes the discarnate with aggressive procedures, he/she can become more violent—insults are not appropriate.

It is my belief and my experience of many years that if a practitioner works with their own Divine Guidance, the Angelic Kingdom and Universal Law, an "exorcism" can be relatively peaceful. We have dealt with many very nasty, violent entities, but we do not have to do it alone.

For those who label possession as being caused by one or more "demonic spirits" or "unclean spirits," it is a abomination to do so. This type of reference is founded in fear and ignorance. There is a poor success rate with many of these primitive clearing methods, and extreme damage and even destruction of human life caused by these types of exorcisms. Some facilitators have been permanently affected and quietly put away in mental institutions after such encounters, including a several priests of the Catholic Church.

I wish to remind anyone doing work in the realm of Spirit that we must abide by the Universal Principles or we are open to the consequences. Doing battle with discarnate spirits has been the traditional method of exorcism for most cultural and religious practitioners. This method is not in harmony with Divine Law and it is totally unnecessary and often dangerous and usually unsuccessful. Working within Divine Law with the assistance of Angelic beings is always beneficial to everyone involved.

Honoring The Dead

In many cultures, past and present, the dead are acknowledged once a year to honor, entertain and communicate with them. Some festivities are held in the cemeteries with a general cleaning and decorating of the graves. This ceremony is known as the "Day of the Dead" in Latin countries. In the Japanese tradition, "Bon" or Urabon festival is a Buddhist tradition. It is referred to as the festival of the souls, to honor the dead. It is the one time of the year for deceased loved ones to visit their earthly families. Food is prepared for them and special lanterns are hung and dancing is part of the celebration. The festival ends with paper lanterns set upon the waters of rivers or the sea, sending the spirits back to their realm. It is also understood that many spirits will take this opportunity complete their death journeys and leave the earthly planes.

To honor the dead I have placed a "soul train" station in my back yard. It is a white wooden table and chair with sign pointing upward with the words painted on it, "Soul Train Station." I asked for angelic escorts to assist me in creating a vortex of release for the deceased and that they tend to the traffic. My house is the location of most of our sessions, so we often have many dead folks coming through. This has been on-going for many years which has turned my property into a large vortex, quite visible in the spirit world. The soul train station is to keep the traffic moving through, away from the living space, to maintain a peaceful environment and to prevent "air traffic" congestion.

Within most cultural practices, exorcism is very common, and has been known to them since times of antiquity and there is an understanding that the spirit world is very full and very interactive with earth humans. It is as normal a process as consulting a doctor for a cold or flu. The affect that non-physical entities or energies can have on embodied humans or animals, mentally, emotionally, physically or spiritually, is understood and accepted into their daily lives and basic concepts of earthly existence.

"If You Want to Know Who You Really Are—First Find Out Who Everyone Else Is, Release them and You're Who's Left!"

The results of a clearing can be subtle or extreme, depending on the type of attachment and the degree of control exerted by those in attachment. The client goes through a shift on all levels. Most say they feel lighter right away. Some require a few days of quiet and rest as they process their experience. For others, the changes are more severe, but the ultimate effects are always for the better.

After a clearing, one client went home to his wife of two months, walked in, looked at her and said, "Who in the hell are you?" The wife heard his story and came for a clearing a week later. They were divorced in a few weeks. As it turned out, a very strong male discarnate (the client's father) had chosen to marry the wife only two weeks after meeting her!

For all clients, there is a healing activated at all levels. The extent of that healing/clearing depends on the client and their willingness to be open to receive the energies and to let go of all that does not serve their highest purpose. For some, a clearing is completely transformational, expanding and lifting them to another level of awareness. We are always available for any follow-up counseling and we always encourage our clients to let us know of the outcome. The results are always an improvement to a greater or lesser degree. Some clients have thanked us for "saving" their lives, sanity, health, money, jobs, relationships, etc.

Dr. Edith Fiore tells of many changes in her patients after a clearing, in her book, The Unquiet Dead. I recall reading about one of her patients, a woman, who went home after a clearing session to find herself repelled by the wardrobe in her closet, which was rather unisex in style. The discarnate that had been released was a male. A new feminine wardrobe was definitely in order.

There are many types of exorcists or practitioners who do this work: priests, ministers, shamans, doctors of psychology and psychiatry, witches, rabbis, psychics and other cultural practitioners. A vital issue regarding exorcism and the methods used lies in the consideration of karmic responsibility through Universal Law and concern for the discarnates involved. They must be identified to clearly understand and release the situation. In more severe cases this can make the difference between doing a successful clearing or not.

In classic mythology, dolphins are the carriers of the souls of the dead to the nether worlds. In Christianity, the dolphin represents the symbol of Christ....nice connection.

Charms And Magic For Prevention?

Beans, nuts and seeds have a history of association with ghosts, souls of the dead and other spirits, probably because they represent little blueprints of life itself. They were used by some cultures as valuable offerings to the dead (to appease them) and were incorporated with great ceremony. Here in Hawaii, the traditional items are fruit or flowers, although some discarnate ancestors have requested fish instead, usually those living near the shore.

All indigenous cultures have methods to ward off ghosts of all types, including evil spirits. These include the use of charms and ceremony ranging from the most simple to the very elaborate. A simple act of crossing one's self or holding up two crossed fingers is a basic gesture. In Hawaii, "ai kukae" (eat shit) is a phrase said to ward off an evil presence. Tossing salt is a custom used widely, as salt represents purification. A ring of salt around a bed in combination with Ti leaf is a variation used in Hawaii.

Many different herbs have been used for protection throughout history. St. John's Wort is one that has been used for centuries to drive out ghosts, elementals, dark witches and the devil. It has a long history as a preventative herb used in seasonal ceremonies to protect crops, livestock, humans, etc., and in exorcism. It is placed at a certain location for protection or to ward off illness or to heal the sick. Certain other natural substances derived from stones or metals are used in formulas or as charms, especially silver. In China a jade amulet is carried on the person to maintain good "joss" (luck or fortune). A wooden octagon frame with a mirror in the center is also used to ward off harm to a household. I use both, as I am fond of things Chinese (past-life memory).

Other examples include black obsidian stone to ward off negative energies, chalcedony stone to carry on one's person. Chalcedony is also carved as the inner cup of a religious chalice that holds the holy water for church ceremonies. This stone is the only one that will not absorb negative energies. Smudging with sage, cedar, eucalyptus or other herbs is a common process to clear dark energy. An iron horseshoe placed upright (visually resembling a cup) over a doorway catches and holds good luck. An iron rod driven into the grave will prevent escape of the spirit within. The wearing of a cross or hanging one somewhere and the wearing of amber or black tourmaline, have also been used for protection.

Tying red fabric or string around the neck of an animal for protection is common in Latin America. The loud ringing of brass bells or discs in Asian cultures or the noise of a rattle or fireworks in Africa, clears negative energy and spirits. I have a "witch ball" hanging in my front porch. I found it in a catalogue. It is purple glass in the form of a ball, with strings of glass through the hollow center. The old European story goes that the bad witches get tangled up in those strings so they cannot enter your home. It is quite pretty and I enjoy the antiquity of the concept. I collect other such items from many cultures. A girl can never have too many charms.

Lighted candles of specific colors have long been used to ward off evil. They are sometimes lit in full circle around the one needing protection or around a corpse to protect it until burial. This practice keeps the spirit of the one in the center contained and prevents evil spirits from taking their soul.

A more elaborate process comes from England. When someone dies all doors, cupboards, and windows in the home are unlocked and opened to let out the spirit of the one who died. Then the corpse is carried out of the home feet first and everyone touches the corpse to prevent haunting in dreams. Some rearrange the bedroom furniture of the deceased during the funeral so if the spirit returns, it won't recognize the room and will leave. The funeral party takes a different route home than the one taken to the funeral to prevent a ghost from following.

I have only touched on this subject and there is a lot of research material available for you to explore. Be sure to wear garlic!

Preparation

One important aspect of our work is that each entity is treated with respect, regardless of their deeds or attitude. All beings have a divine right to exist. It is not our right to judge or criticize. That is not what our work is about. Yes, we have personal opinions about a given situation, but our personal peeves are not appropriate in these sessions—we must remain impersonal, with compassion and understanding. Yes, my tongue has slipped a few times, but I always give apology for any emotional "seepage."

Most discarnates are very willing to share basic information about themselves, but we must always use discernment when dealing with those who are in strong manipulation mode. These entities want to remain attached to a client they don't want to release. We request containment for them, from Archangel Michael. This allows us to communicate with them in safety.

We always work within Universal Law, which is why we have strong support from the angelic assistants. We utilize other tools and processes (see Toolbox) when there is a need, or to release karmatic contracts, agreements or cords, which are usually unknown to our clients, as these often relate to past life situations.

When I request that a violent entity be placed into containment, it is done. We often encounter those who have the ability to camouflage or hide their presence. Our senses must detect that something is not clear and then we ask for angelic assistance to reveal it. Some discarnates are dangerous and try to stop or harm us, but it is our responsibility to be in proper working modality, detached from fear.

We do ongoing maintenance to remain in balance by using the tools and monitoring our state of being in body, mind and spirit. We live our philosophy. We support and monitor each other. We conduct regular inquiries and do clearings for ourselves when necessary. As a working group, we made that commitment to our work, ourselves and to each other many years ago, personally and professionally. There can be no separation.

We are eclectic in our work. This gives flexibility and compatibility to all we work with, regardless of culture, race or religion. We honor all the deities of various peoples and we intend no harm to anyone. This is one very important rule, which is our basis of focus. This is the only "sin" within the Huna philosophy of the ancient Hawaiian culture. Stated simply, it is, "Never to intend harm to the self or another." This is one of the most important of the Universal Principles.

As many as nine of us have done a particular job (large hotels), although there are always two, and sometimes three of us for most clearings. There is at least one who channels the entities although sometimes it is the clients themselves who channel. I usually do the questioning and verbal invocations. We each do what we do the best, even though we are all sensitives.

Setting The Appointment

A call comes in. I ask the caller to explain why they feel they need a clearing. It is important to treat the client with respect, regardless of what they are telling me. Their experience is REAL for them and we must honor that. I ask certain routine questions, such as: Are you using drugs (including prescribed) or alcohol? Are there any health conditions? Have there been any deaths, crises or disputes recently?

I always eliminate the obvious possibilities first. When there is question about the symptoms, we "tune-in" psychically to verify the need for a clearing. We discourage anyone from going through a clearing if they choose to remain addicted to drugs or alcohol, simply because it would be futile. A complete release is usually accomplished in one session, but those clients would still be very open for more attachment in a couple of days. We rarely have that type of request, although we have assisted those who want to heal their addiction if it appears to be caused or exacerbated by attachments.

Activation

Once we agree on an appointment date, I always activate the energies over the phone. This includes calling upon angelic assistance to create a "vortex" of Light energy for release of those souls who are ready, now, and protection from those who may try to prevent a release. I request that all violent or manipulative entities or energies be placed into containment, now.

I call upon angelic guides to assist those who may be in confusion, to help them see the reality of their situation. I speak directly to those who may be attached and ask all to remain calm until the appointed time where each one will have opportunity to speak. I assure them we are here to assist, we are not here to criticize, harm or force them to do anything. I give thanks for the angelic assistance and that of our personal guides, and so be it!

The reason for the telephone activation is because of past experience with discarnates who caused great disruption for the client right after making the appointment or as they are preparing to leave for the appointment. Of course they can hear us. That is why they react. In one instance a bathroom mirror suddenly broke and fell as the client was standing in front of it preparing to leave her house.

Another, more serious incident, involved a client who was in a car accident while driving to the appointment. Fortunately, it was not a serious accident. Even with the activation, there can be emotional interference caused by the discarnate affecting the client or ourselves. We are always aware of possible sabotage and prepare ourselves at the time of the appointment. We automatically tune-in to any unusual activity or feelings that may occur prior to a session.

It is common for discarnates to have a higher awareness than they had attained at the time of their death. There are a few reasons for this. The discarnate has been in the astral for a long time and has acquired knowledge through observing or through the influence of another discarnate who is with or near them. Their own higher guidance is also influencing their awareness. Another contributing factor can be the activation process itself, which calls in guidance specifically. The time span between phone call and appointment can be two days to a week or more. The age of the discarnate has little to do with communication, even with babies and children, as we are dealing with most of them at a soul/spirit (adult) level of communication.

The Inquiry

The client arrives. We sit in circle and open the session with the Christ Light Invocation (see Toolbox). We then call upon our personal Divine Guidance and ask the client to do the same. Finally, we call upon Archangel Michael and begin communication. I ask those in attachment to choose among themselves who will come forward, in what order, and if there are any groups to please choose a representative to speak for them, "And will the first person come forward and identify yourself please?"

As we begin communication with the entities present, I inquire about some basic information during the conversation. I ask how old they are? Are they aware they are deceased? Why and when did they attach to the client? Did they know them before they died? Do they have any questions? etc. We also ask the client if they have any questions to ask the discarnate(s). The rest of the inquiry varies according to the situation. In some cases, mediation is required to bring resolve. Some spirits require counseling about their state of being and what release means. Ho'oponopono ceremony is done between the client and all who are in attachment prior to their release.

The Release

After all appropriate processes or ceremonies are completed the spirits are released with the assistance of escorts from Archangel Michael, safely into Divine Light as we thank them for speaking with us and wish them well. Very few of them ever refuse to be released. If they do refuse, they are placed into containment for contemplation. Divine Guidance is provided for them and they are left in the hands of Archangel Michael.

All are given these two choices. No one remains attached unless there is mutual agreement and it is to the highest purpose of both the discarnate and the host.

The earthly bodies of many discarnates were deteriorated by illness or damaged by the cause of death. They often view their body as it was, in that damaged condition. I assure them they will have their own perfect body as they are released into the Light.

One Hawaiian warrior would not leave without his body. The warriors of those times made great effort to perfect and maintain their bodies. It was very much a part of their identity, like Olympic athletes, models, or ballet dancers. I asked Guidance if an angelic escort could carry it for him (it never hurts to ask), and the reply was yes. They all ascended together…

There are other specific situations or requests that have been made for release into Light. A discarnate child, who was very frightened, asked me to take him by the hand to the doorway at the end of the tunnel. I agreed and it was beautiful. The "tunnel" itself is quite beautiful. We see it as a long, wide tunnel with beautiful, swirling pastel colors of Light. At the other end is a very bright white Light—that is the doorway.

Another interesting request for release involved a wizard who requested a chariot with "proper escorts." It was provided, in grandeur with a royal blue and heavily gilded chariot and a wonderful robe for the wizard himself. He wasn't particularly thrilled, however because he truly expected it.

A rather humorous release was requested by my father, five years after his death (he had remained to tend to some unfinished issues). He said, "You know this angel stuff isn't my style." I said, "Yes daddy, what would you like to do." He wanted to be shot out of a cannon! And so it was…A huge cannon was produced and he proceeded with his release. I was quite surprised at his choice, and it is still the strangest request we have had so far.

Another release arrangement called for a fleet of Harley Davidson motorcycles (deceased bikers are usually in groups). The bikes "presented" are always quite beautiful, brand new with lots of chrome. The bikers are always "blown away" with the presentation. Of course, all bikers go to heaven…eventually.

We release many groups of people: whole villages, groups of warriors from every culture and time period, soldiers, and often their enemy troops and civilians who were all killed in the same area. When we have multiple groups like this, they usually remain segregated as they are released. We have released many hundreds from World War II, Nazis, Jews and others. We have released many from the Spanish Inquisition and other horrible group tragedies, including airplane crashes and the Jonestown Massacre.

We never really know who or what we will discover until we are in session. It is important to keep an open mind, as we are dealing with humanity in general. Even though they are deceased, they too are our clients. We include all animals in each session, which sometimes includes pets. If we are dealing with ocean death or coastal areas, the release often includes whales, dolphins and lots of sailors, especially here in Hawaii.

The hosts (our embodied clients) and the discarnates that are attached to them come from all areas of society and profession, from those with minimal formal education to professionals and those who are quite famous. There are some who are in front of the public eye and others who are not. In the course of hundreds of clearings we have encountered kings and queens, demons and saints and many others from history. Some are reincarnated as our embodied clients and others were deceased and requested our assistance. We have conversed with the deceased from civilizations unknown to historians and with those form ancient civilizations whose only remaining trace are some artifacts. We have been shown ancient ceremonies and lifestyles, probably enough for another book. And written history is not as accurate as it could be.

We have worked with many situations in the course of the clearings. Some of these involve escrows that are being blocked, difficult court cases of various types, business ventures, political situations and criminal activities. We have encountered people who were lost in time/space. In one of those cases we found several soldiers who were "blown" out of their time/space by an experiment in 1946 in the U.S. We called for assistance to return them…

The Session

The following cases are chosen from the many hundred cases we have had over the years. They are exact transcripts from the audio tapes of those sessions. Two of the transcripts are complete and the others are excerpts from more extensive sessions. Very few people have just one discarnate. I have tried to show a variety of situations. To preserve confidentiality, I have changed all of the names of the embodied clients. The names of the discarnates are written as given to us. They always have the choice of giving their real name or initials, or none at all.

The channels for these sessions are Roy, Suzanne and Susie. When they are speaking exactly (channeling) as the discarnate, it will be in italics. When they are relating what they see or hear the discarnate say, it will be in regular text. There really is no specific timing for either mode, the communication simply flows in this way, although sometimes the channel will relate rather than let the discarnate speak directly. This can often expedite the process when the discarnate is emotional, irate or swearing.

Our sessions usually take place in my home office. They last from about forty-five minutes to an hour. We sit in circle on a carpeted floor with low lighting and a tape recorder in the center of the circle on the floor.

CASE 1: The client is Milly's brother Toby, who lives in California. This is an absentee clearing. The symptoms are drug and alcohol abuse, suicide attempts and several life-threatening accidents. This appointment was made one week prior to the clearing. The day before the appointment, Milly called me and said that her brother had shot himself in the chest and was in the hospital. She asked if we could move the appointment ahead to that evening, and we did. Milly is present, representing her brother.

IN SESSION:

SUZ: Describes there is a curse-like energy, involving a male discarnate in some kind of dueling situation.

JERI: I call the male discarnate forward—please give us your first name.

SUZ: *Eric.*

JERI: How old are you?

SUZ: *Twenty-three.*

JERI: Are you aware that you no longer have your physical body?

SUZ: *Quite!*

JERI: And were you killed in a battle of some kind?

SUZ: *Yes, but he was very sneaky about it!*

JERI: Could it be that you're just a tiny bit angry that he got the best of you?

SUZ: *A tiny bit!!*

JERI: I could be wrong, but isn't all fair in love and war? Sort of like, "May the best man win?" Or was it different?

SUZ: *It was different.*

JERI: Did he do something that would be considered cheating?

SUZ: *Absolutely! Why do you think I've wasted my time for all these years?*

JERI: Well, that was going to be my next question. How much more time are you going to waste?

SUZ: *Until he dies by my hands!*

JERI: Did you attempt again this morning?

SUZ: *Yes!*

JERI: And other times as well?

SUZ: *Yes!*

JERI: Is this really necessary? It seems to me that it is costing you. You could have gone on and had, who knows what other sort of lifetimes, or been shown the whole picture of your situation and choices for your future path.

SUZ: He's shaking his head, he doesn't understand.

JERI: That is what is available to you. You are not stuck in this place or attached to this person's body, except through your own anger—you do have a choice.

SUZ: *It's a vow I made.*

JERI: You can change that too.

SUZ: *I've never broken a vow before.*

JERI: Well, you wouldn't be breaking a vow—you would be altering a vow. It seems that hundreds of years have gone by—how long is a vow like that good for? You have put in an awfully long time on it.

SUZ: *And not successfully.*

JERI: Is that really what is most important? It seems that you are in self-sacrifice mode. I'm sure you are causing some pain and disruption, and now destruction in Toby's life—but you are literally preventing your own—preventing it! You're not even in your own body—you're using someone else's! So, after all these years, is it possible that perhaps you would like to change a few things?

SUZ: He started to say, "Now, see here!" But he kind of looked around and realized you were right.

JERI: Here's an alternative plan that I will present to you. Usually, there is a very strong karmatic situation in killing, and one person is due some kind of payment or balance. As you move into the Light, you can get organized and make a choice for your next life. Yes, you have other lives ahead of you with new body, new everything. Same person, just a new movie, and you choose your own character. Often, what happens is that people (even enemies) choose another life together to bring balance to their relationship.

Since you decided to be in the astral plane, attach yourself to this body and not become reincarnated, you can't be here in this life with him.

SUZ: *So, I need to kill him from here!*

JERI: Well, if you insist, I can't tell you what to do. What if, in a life before the last one, you were together and you murdered him in cold blood or butchered his whole family? What if killing you was balancing the score, so to speak? Do you see how this can be? We don't always see our reality from these earthbound planes. You are now in the lower astral which kind of blocks your view.

If you wish to go into the higher planes, to be released into the Light, then there are guides there to assist you with something like a movie about your past, your present and your possible future. This is so you can have a clear understanding of what has happened to you. Does that make sense to you?

SUZ: *Yes.*

JERI: The worst thing that can happen is that you reincarnate, meet him in an alley and just shoot him in cold blood.

SUZ: *Worst?*

JERI: Well, the least, I should say. The "highest" thing that could happen is that you may change your mind.

SUZ: *So why are you helping him?*

JERI: We are helping both of you. If we didn't want to help you, I wouldn't have spent the last ten minutes explaining anything—I would have asked the angels come in, stick you in a cage and leave you there.

We believe there are no victims in higher reality there is always a bigger picture. We like to try to see what that is for the sake of those we assist, and ourselves, for understanding. You will be shown the answers.

SUZ: He's thinking, since it didn't work this time, maybe it will work from "there" (after release).

JERI: Yes, could be—but we will also make a request from this end for protection for Toby. It is simply not to be that you kill him in this way, or it would have already happened. If I were you I'd want to find out why.

I don't know what condition Toby is in at this time (asking Milly). Is he out of the critical stage?

MILLY: I think so.

SUZ: Eric feels he is not going to die—he feels like he (Eric) has failed again.

JERI: I don't feel he is going to die either.

MILLY: No, nor do I.

JERI: So it seems the "gods" are not letting it happen this way. So why not take a chance? If you are that kind of warrior—I sense you probably have a great deal of courage—to trust us enough to go into that tunnel and sail toward that Light. It does represent your freedom.

At this time we request escorts from Archangel Michael, just to come and stand (or float, as it were), and wait for your decision.

SUZ: He is moving toward, but he is not verbalizing. I think he has decided to go ahead and give it a try. The statement about his courage kind of did it.

JERI: Eric, we pay our respects to you and thank you for speaking with us. If you are ready, the escorts are there. We wish you well. We now request escorts from Archangel Michael to come and assist Eric, safely into Divine Light, and we wish you well.

This was a very stubborn discarnate, as you can tell. We released a few others after Eric left. Toby survived his gunshot wound, which had been point-blank into the chest, although the doctors were amazed. We cleared this client in 1992, and to this day, Toby has no problem with drugs or alcohol and has not had any more accidents or suicide attempts.

This case was the one that prompted us to do an activation/protection on the phone, at the time of setting all future appointments, for obvious reasons.

CASE 2: This is an excerpt from a clearing for Jason and Tory who are husband and wife. We have already released several discarnates from Tory and we released more from Jason after this. They have come to clear unwanted outer influence creating friction in their relationship. The channel for this session is Roy.

IN SESSION: as Roy tunes-in to the picture.

ROY: Jason, there is a motorcycle guy—he's been hanging around with you since you were age eighteen, and he's been distorting your life in regard to your understanding of who you are and what you can contribute to yourself, as well as to the world. His name is Aaron. He was killed in a gang fight, he says New York City. For a time he bounced from person to person but found you most amiable, so he latched on and really does not want to leave.

JERI: Does he wish to communicate? I would like to speak to him.

ROY: *What do you want?*

JERI: We are here to assist you, not to give you a hard time. Are you aware that you no longer have your own physical body?

ROY: *Huh, you wanna tell me some more? What is this about?*

JERI: Well, check it out—look down—are those your legs?

ROY: *No.*

JERI: Is that your chest?

ROY: *No.*

JERI: Is that your hair?

ROY: *No.*

JERI: All of what you are looking at belongs to this man named Jason.

ROY: *You're kidding me!*

JERI: He is sitting here with us. Now, just to see what the truth of it is, I would like you to think back. In your memory, there is a picture, a record of exactly what happened that caused you to decease your physical body. Let's look back there now…Tell me what you see…What happened to you?

ROY: *Oh, oh! Those guys knifed me four times!*

JERI: How many of them?

ROY: *Eight of em!*

JERI: Were you by yourself?

ROY: *No, I had twelve other guys with me.*

JERI: Was it like a gang thing?

ROY: *Yep! Oh, oh!*

JERI: Can you see what happened now? Were you the only one that was killed?

ROY: *I see five other people.*

JERI: Do you see them near you now?

ROY: *Yep! Well, whataya know?*

JERI: Are they from your side?

ROY: *My side and their side.*

JERI: That's cheating, huh?

ROY: *Yep! Ya know, I was wondering why I have had such distraction sometimes—they're all with me!*

JERI: Would you or they mind, if you were their representative for this meeting?

ROY: *O.K., they're all nodding their heads.*

JERI: Have you all witnessed the release of people that took place earlier?

ROY: *Yep.*

JERI: So, how is everyone feeling? Are you all ready to be released so you can move on?

ROY: *Yep.*

JERI: We ask you now to gather together, as we call upon escorts from Archangel Michael…

ROY: *Well, it's mighty nice of them to provide us with motorcycles.*

JERI: Those are your favorite things, aren't they?

ROY: *Right on!*

JERI: I think you will all enjoy this ride—it will be different.

ROY: *Well, see you later and thanks for the ride, Jason. It's been fun, more than you'll ever know.*

JERI: Just imagine Jason, someone who's been riding with you since you were eighteen (now in his thirties). We ask you all to gather together as we now request that you be released, safely into Divine Light. We thank you for speaking with us and we wish you well.

This case is a good example of how discarnates can influence one's life for a long time. It is also important to realize that being a discarnate in attachment (or not) is also part of "life's" journey for many. It is a continuation of earth-life that is unfinished, where there is more to experience, albeit, without a physical body. Some discarnates remain in the lower astral, interacting with earthlings, for decades or longer. Some of them are helpful or benevolent and others are harmful or malevolent. The type of journey anyone takes is a personal choice. The rules do not change, each of us creates our own reality whether one is the "host" or the "discarnate" and often that journey is with each other.

I will now share a very sad story of two people who had a long journey together, one dead but attached to the other, who was embodied. Two teenagers were dating each other in high school. The girl became pregnant. The boy agreed to marry her and be responsible for his new family. As time passed, the wife was told by a trusted friend that her new husband was bi-sexual. The young Catholic girl was devastated beyond repair. A short time later, the boy came home after work to find the bathroom door locked. He became alarmed when there was no answer from his wife. He broke the door down and found her in the bathtub, with little prayer cards and candles lining the rim of the tub. She was dead—she had killed herself. She left a horrible note of blame as her last statement.

Years later, in session, as we tuned-in to clear the husband, we could see that the girl literally jumped onto her husband as he stood at the tub in horror. The girl's only intention from that point on was to kill her husband. The boy later developed AIDS and was enduring various treatments when he came to us for the clearing. The wife absolutely refused to release, refused to go into the Light, had no concern for any karma she was creating for herself. The husband was so full of guilt he could not release her completely. We requested she be placed into "containment" and so it was, but he continued to allow her to influence him telepathically. That tragic husband died about one year later. These two people "lived" in this mode for about eighteen years.

CASE 3: This session was a personal release for a friend who had passed away two weeks prior. Assisting me as the channel, and a mutual friend, is Susie. Our deceased friend is Bonnie, a friend outside of our group of practitioners. Bonnie was not familiar with metaphysics in general, nor the philosophy we embrace.

IN SESSION:

JERI: I call Bonnie forward and ask if we can visit for a while.

SUSIE: It's Bonnie, she looks happy.

JERI: Good evening Bonnie. Have you completed your rounds, your farewells?

SUSIE: She has, but she gets a little hung up on the sadness.

JERI: Yes, this is part of your process. Sarah (a friend), in particular, is very upset because she didn't get to say goodbye.

SUSIE: *Oh hon, don't get caught up in human emotions, you helped me more than you'll ever know.* Other personal issues were then discussed.

JERI: Are you ready to be released into the Light?

SUSIE: She is trying to get away.

JERI: I sense you don't feel worthy. Why?

SUSIE: She wasn't truthful with her family—she wouldn't let them share her pain—she had to be strong (she died of cancer).

JERI: To the best of my recollection, you didn't behave any differently than before you were sick—you have always "had to be strong." As you are released into the Light, there will be guides there to help you.

SUSIE: She said she has had three meetings already.

JERI: You will still be able to communicate with your family in spirit. So, are you ready to release now?

SUSIE: You mean open up the white door and see what's behind it?

JERI: Yes.

SUSIE: She's afraid she will go to purgatory (Bonnie is Catholic).

JERI: There's no such thing!

SUSIE: *Can you show me a preview, in case I can't come back?*

JERI: We can do something almost as good. I am calling an escort from Archangel Michael right now, to show you what is there. As you feel their energy coming closer, you will become more calm and joyful

SUSIE: She is saying "Hail Mary's" at 80 miles an hour and, I'm sorry I ate meat on Friday! She is feeling major guilt. She is in a black box of some kind and says she's stuck.

JERI: Bonnie, I would like you to open the box and allow the angel to take your hand.

SUSIE: Ooohhh!! She's in the damn coffin and can't get out!

JERI: Allow the angel to help you.

SUSIE: *There's all this dirt…I can't!*

JERI: You can open the box…just raise your foot and kick it as hard as you can and come right out the top!

SUSIE: Yes, she's out, thank God.

JERI: Is that better?

SUSIE: She hates that dress.

JERI: Take it off! We ask guidance to present you with another, tear the old one up if you wish.

SUSIE: She's going to put it back in the box—she's being very neat about it (that's new) and she has a garland of flowers, a haku (head) lei in her hair and looks much younger now.

JERI: And one of the neat things about where you're going is that you will have your very own perfect Light body and not an ounce overweight, and in perfect condition.

SUSIE: She feels pain in her heart for her children (two under fifteen).

JERI: Would you like to request angelic companions for them, to assist and comfort them?

SUSIE: *Oh! Could we please?*

JERI: We request this now please.

SUSIE: Some people in green robes are here (spirit guides).

JERI: And if you are ready now.

SUSIE: She says it feels wonderful to be free. My leg hurts though, the one she kicked the lid off with! (Susie is feeling sympathetic pain from Bonnie)

JERI: That will pass. We now request escorts from Archangel Michael to come and assist our dear friend Bonnie, safely into Divine Light. We request Divine protection and guidance for her family. We love you Bonnie, aloha.

This case is an example of how guilt and negative programming (purgatory) can inhibit a peaceful passing. Most people do not have friends who will assist them once they die, to complete their death journey. It would be wonderful and I encourage anyone to learn to do this. If we had not done a release for Bonnie, she could have been stuck in that coffin for an indefinite period of time. It is also true that many who die need to spend some time in the earthly plane to visit family or friends, to take care of unfinished business and always to attend their own funeral services. We always wait for a minimum of seven days before helping with a release. If a discarnate needs to stay longer, we simply request Angelic escorts to help and protect them while they take care of their affairs.

CASE 4: This session excerpt is from a clearing for Danny, a Viet Nam War veteran. He wanted to release any negative influences interfering with his present relationships. The channel is Suzanne.

IN SESSION: There were many warring factions attached, including Native Americans, gang members, a female suicide, a small Vietnamese village that was burned by napalm and others. A very interesting discarnate was Quan Li, a wartime Viet Nam civilian.

SUZ: There is a very agitated man here. He is connected to Danny but he doesn't know if it's because it was Danny or someone else near him who took his ear. He is very afraid because of his belief, that he won't be reborn (reincarnated) without his ear. His name is Quan Li.

NOTE: A common belief in numerous cultures is that any missing body part prevents the soul from moving on (into Light), and can even mean damage to the soul.

JERI: Good evening Quan Li. Would you allow us to assist you? We call upon angelic assistance to come now and show you, although your physical ear may be gone, your ethereal ear, your true ear is still here…I ask them to show you this now.

SUZ: It is interesting, he's hooked into you, Danny, because of his perception that you were the one—though it could have been any one of a group of people in the picture I'm getting (American soldiers raided a bar/restaurant).

JERI: A lot of times discarnates jump onto their attacker in retaliation, or onto whom they believe it to be. So, how are you feeling now, Quan Li, about the reality of your condition?

SUZ: He is kind of sad because he is now aware that something he was taught in his culture is not true.

JERI: It was partially a truth. If you had something missing in the ethereal body there would be a problem. As with many beliefs in the earth-life, they have been watered down and distorted through centuries of variable translation. No harm has truly been done except for your fear, and we are sorry for that. Perhaps it is something you can learn from, if you can now release and let it go. Can you do that?

SUZ: He (Quan Li]) is willing to do the forgiveness process that you did before (with other discarnates in this session).

JERI: I ask now, if Divine guidance can clarify for you, whether or not it was actually Danny, who cut off your ear, yes or no. This is so you can be clear in your heart about that. You do not need to give us the answer, just that you have been shown the truth.

SUZ: He is not sure. Danny's was the last face he saw as he died (due to the severing of his jugular vein with a knife). That is all he knows for sure.

JERI: Then it is not an issue at this time. You will be shown as you move into the higher vibration. So, at this moment Quan Li, if you would simply direct your attention to whomever is responsible.

SUZ: He would be honored if each would forgive the other on behalf of everyone in that battle.

JERI: We now make that request and we are glad for all of you. You have had some time (since the war) to think about it all, which is probably what you needed before completing your death journeys—and to observe what you have seen as you have been traveling with this one (Danny), who was your enemy.

On behalf of Quan Li, we now invoke the entire Ho'oponopono Process between himself and all others involved in this situation, through all time/space and dimensional frequency. We request that all disharmonious energies between them, now be transmuted into pure Light. Quan Li, do you ask for and give, in return, forgiveness between yourself and all who are involved?

SUZ: *Yes*

JERI: We ask the same question of anyone else who wishes to participate—make your statement of forgiveness now.

SUZ: Most all of them do.

JERI: So be it, it is done. We now request Divine blessing for each and every soul/spirit involved. We ask you all to gather together as we call upon escorts from Archangel Michael to come now and assist each one of you safely into Divine Light. We request that all animals be included in this process. We give thanks to all Divine beings who assist us. It is complete.

This situation was very unfortunate because our client was dying of cancer caused by chemicals he was exposed to during the war. Treatment and healing were difficult because his life force was being drained by all of the discarnates attached to him from all factions of the event, the enemies, the civilians, the comrades and all the negative emotions connected to it. This is common with soldiers in war. If a clearing could be done for those who return from war, their recovery and ability to function in peacetime would be greatly enhanced. They would not be carrying the "war" with them in such a direct manner. They would only be left with their own memories—and all memory fades with time, that is nature's way.

CASE 5: This was a situation where a married couple had enlisted the services of a Cuban voodoo type of practitioner (Cora) to enhance their relationship. They went to her separately several times. The husband (Hasan) asked that he and his wife be strong together, but the wife (Belinda) asked that she could have complete control over the husband. The voodoo woman did not reveal this to the husband. She realized she could get more mileage (money) out of the wife, so she focused on her desires.

Hasan became severely dysfunctional emotionally, mentally and physically. He could not sleep without nightmares. He was riddled with fear, he could not be in a dark room and his sanity was slipping away. Belinda had also changed drastically. The couple was separated at the time of the session, but Hasan wanted to be with her again.

All of this took place in Florida. Various other family members had gone to Cora for her services, in the past. Hasan called a friend in Hawaii and the friend told him to get away and come to stay with him. The friend said he knew someone who may be able to help. The channel for this session is Roy.

IN SESSION: Hasan is very nervous. Roy and I had been shielding strongly since the appointment was made a few days ago. We could feel the very strong energies that were being used in the spell. Hasan is also a sensitive, but has been shut down completely. He speaks with strong Spanish accent.

ROY: There are little tornados moving all over the room, about nine of them.

JERI: I call upon the source/creator of this energy.

ROY: A lady with black hair—looks like early 30's—her name is Tina. She's angry and says *why are you bothering us?*

JERI: We are here to assist Hasan. Are you discarnate or in body?

ROY: She's laughing—she's in body.

JERI: Are you connected to the practitioner who placed the spell on Hasan?

ROY: Instead of herself (Cora) working, she has four or five other people working with her. This woman has black (energy) entities attached and not all human. She is now changing form (shape-shifting), resembling Medusa, in skeletal form (trying to scare us).

JERI: Hasan, I need to ask you, do you give permission for any attachments from Cora to remain?

HASAN: No, nothing!

JERI: No you no longer give the practitioner, Cora, permission to continue any work upon you at all—you wish to cancel your original request for her service?

HASAN: Yes!

JERI: And we state the reason. That her service was not for Hasan's highest purpose, as he believed it was.

ROY: You've got to do better—she has developed three different personalities—like duplicate energies of herself.

JERI: I speak to you now, Tina, do you have any kind of connection to Hasan, from this life or past life?

ROY: She said past life.

JERI: On behalf of Hasan, we now invoke the entire Ho'oponopono process between himself and you and all that is connected to you, through all time/space and dimensional frequency. And now Tina, you must completely disconnect in a safe manner, on all levels.

ROY: She is feeling this one.

JERI: And since you are still in body, we have no call to offer release to you, but if you wish, we can request Divine Guidance.

ROY: She is laughing, she says, *we have Divine Guidance.* While we're at it, there is Ruby, Katalina and there's Dona Teresa.

JERI: Are these embodied or discarnate

ROY: Embodied.

JERI: Helpers?

ROY: Yes. There's also an older lady that is attached to Cora, a discarnate who is using a lot of forces. She knows Hasan is trying to get loose.

JERI: At this time, we complete the clearing with any other embodied attachments—all of you come forward now (we completed with the rest of them).

ROY: Hasan needs to cut cords.

JERI: We call upon Hasan's Divine Guidance to assist him now in that process.

ROY: A major hold on first, second, third and fourth chakras (root, sexual/creative, emotional and heart centers). The seven knots have to be dissolved and a reversal of all the processes Cora made to invoke the spell—as well as requesting that the spirit of the bird is released into Light. Did it fly? (asking Hasan—a bird was part of the ceremony).

HASAN: She was too heavy to fly. I don't see her die, she start to run around. The feet were cut and there was a lot of blood, a white bird.

JERI: We'll do that when we get to Cora. So are we complete with the embodied ones?

ROY: It is in process, so complete with Cora.

JERI: We now call forward the soul/spirit of Cora. We are now informing you that Hasan completely cancels any permission he gave you to do any work for him whatsoever!

ROY: She is calling in all her forces.

JERI: I'll bet she is. We have already asked that you be placed into containment until this session is completed (Hasan is very uncomfortable).

ROY: She is trying to pull his (Hasan) strings.

HASAN: She will lock me!

JERI: You will be alright.

HASAN: No, no want!

JERI: Don't give any attention to her. I ask guidance now if there are any past karmic ties between Hasan and Cora.

ROY: Him and his whole family.

HASAN: Did she lie to me all the time? She has been against me, yes? I not forget her!

JERI: She is an enemy from your past lives, but you will probably find that you did things to her as well, and so on. The only way to really clear and stop the negative karma...

HASAN: Forgive her?

JERI: Yes, if you can feel that in your heart.

HASAN: My heart say, forgive her.

JERI: And do you also ask for forgiveness as well?

HASAN: Yes, for me and my family.

JERI: (We completed ho'oponopono)...and in accordance with Divine Law, you, Cora, must now release from Hasan, his family and his wife Belinda (we continued with severing aka cords). We will now complete the release by undoing the spell. We direct Cora now to trace back to the beginning and release all of the spell work you did.

NOTE: Cora's spell included using colored ribbons tied with knots, the sacrifice of a white bird at the ocean, candles, herbs and other spell objects and invocations.

JERI: We have no jurisdiction to release any discarnates from Cora, so we leave them to themselves. We now call in the soul/spirit of Belinda (Hasan's wife) and ask if we can be of assistance.

ROY: She is very connected to Cora and the others.

JERI: Yes, Belinda is being manipulated by Cora. This is so Cora can continue to get more money for services from her.

HASAN: Yes, she always coming to her!

ROY: Yes, she wants your money.

HASAN: Can you help her?

JERI: Yes, we have activated a release and blessing, but only to the degree that Belinda is willing to accept it.

ROY: Cora was also trying to fragment Hasan's soul energy by pulling part of it out into the astral. We need to pull it back.

JERI: Hasan, you must now open your heart and crown, carefully, and call any extended soul energy back unto your self. We request Divine Guidance to oversee Cora, as we ask her to complete the work she was instructed to do, now!

ROY: Cora is going through a kind of fit.

JERI: Cora is having a fit?

ROY: Her body is shaking and she doesn't want to do this, but she has no choice.

JERI: Well, with all the shit you're into madam, it's a wonder you don't have arthritis! No offense intended (one of my slips).

ROY: There is a big fight to avoid clearing, but they know they must, and have no permission to reconnect.

JERI: We thank Divine Guidance for "encouraging" them. The ancestors have been waiting for this help. They couldn't do it on their own. And by the way Cora, are you aware of the kind of karmatic situation you are creating for yourself?

ROY: Yes, but she says it's being taken care of.

JERI: Taken care of?

ROY: She doesn't understand that all it does is compound. She thinks someone else is taking care of it for her.

JERI: Well, I would like Divine Guidance to show you now, that it is NOT being taken care of by anyone. You are being lied to, Cora, by those who manipulate you. You will ultimately have to deal with all of it yourself, unfortunately.

ROY: Hasan needs assistance in pulling his soul energy back into his body. It's like it's halfway in.

JERI: Hasan, if you would now open and fill your body with Divine Love/Light energy from your god-self, through your crown. Can you see the gold sparkling flecks within it?

HASAN: Yes, exactly, I see it.

JERI: Good. Allow it to fill your body, calling in your soul energy. Inhale, as you bring it in.

HASAN: It is coming in, kind of like a snake, inside the light in my body
JERI: Good. Receive it—breathe it in.
HASAN: What about my wife?
JERI: (she gave permission and we completed the clearing and reintegration of soul energy, for Belinda). This has been like a barrel full of garter snakes looking for water!
ROY: There is golden/white light all around both of you now. It is complete.
JERI: Focus now, Hasan, on your future and a loving relationship with your wife, as long as you do not bring others in with spells and such. Witchcraft is real, Voodoo is real, spells and curses are real!
NOTE: Hasan was married before. Then, after that divorce, he went to a Muslim witch (he is Arab/Colombian) from Africa to clear the bad vibes (his term) from that marriage. That seemed to work fine. Then Hasan's brother went to Cora for some personal problems. He became ill and is still having even more problems. Next, Hasan's wife went to Cora, and the rest you know.

We suggested that he tell his family about what happened, and that he be more careful in choosing his witches. Hasan was a new person as we closed the session. He said he could see for the first time in a long time. He was beside himself with joy. As he was leaving, he grabbed Roy, (who is about 5'9") and gave him a very strong bear hug (Hasan is about 6'2") of intense gratitude, which squished the air right out of his lungs, leaving ribs intact, thank god.

This was an extreme case compared to most, but rather common in the category of spells and curses. In some other curse cases, we have encountered Palauan (a kingdom in the South Pacific) witchcraft, which took the life of a boy of ten years of age. The Palauan craft is primitive and very strong. Their forefathers were head hunters and cannibals and they view death in a very different way than we do. A more recent case involved three witches is Greece. When practitioners work in the number of three, it is very powerful. There is also great empowerment when they work on their own ancestral lands. They have reinforcement of the ancestors and the potency of the cultural saturation of the environment at that location. It is very common in many cultures to consult a practitioner for many things. There is nothing wrong with that it is a part of all of our ancestral practice. We do suggest that each of you choose your witches carefully!

CASE 6: This is one of two cases in the book that is a full session. The very nature of this case is why I have included it in full, as you will see. The client is Jesse, in his mid forties, a handsome fellow and soft-spoken. He had been having great difficulties with his teenage daughter and was experiencing increased block-age of his chosen pursuits. He knew it was some kind of astral interference. The channel is Roy.

IN SESSION: We opened with the usual ritual and I called the first person forward…

ROY: *You, you, you!!! Do you know what you did to me, many, many, many years ago? I know you can't hear me or feel me and I can't touch you and I can't do any-thing to your daughter or your son now* (she is in containment), *because there is this protection around you. But do you know what you did to me? I know part of this is my fault because I made this promise to you that I would stay and you could use me, in many lifetimes. But you didn't hear me when I cursed you and decided to attach to you for more lifetimes to punish you. Your other* lifetimes were as screwy as this, and you didn't know it. This time I used your daughter, but now you found out, so I can't do anything. What's the matter with you anyhow?

JERI: Do you wish to explain to him what he did to you?

ROY: *Sure. He was about fifty-something. I idolized him. I came to him looking for help and he helped to take care of my kitty when I was about twelve. From then, I idolized him and wanted to stay with him. Then at age eighteen, my parents kicked me out of the house, so I went to live with him. He became my lover and we had great fun. He would change himself into this beautiful young man, cause he was a wiz-ard—and I was a beautiful young lady. As time went on, he taught me some of his magic and he used me in some of his experiments. He would still be able to become the beautiful young man, but I aged and he could not turn me into the beautiful young lady to match him. In the end, he went out and chased other women and kept me ugly and old, still using me in experiments. He could live for several hundred years and I could only live to one hundred and fifty. I withered away. As my soul left my body, I cursed him and said I would be with him forever! So here I am.*

JERI: I would like to ask you about yourself, leaving him aside and forgetting about him for the moment. What would you like for yourself? There is an oppor-tunity for you now, to go onto a new path and have a new life.

ROY: *I guess what I really want is to have the beautiful young man that he always turned himself into, and all the love and protection and all the beautiful times we had together. Not all the ugliness—that was at the end of our great and wonderful rela-tionship—was there in the beginning that started out so beautifully.*

JERI: Obviously, that is in the past, but it does not mean that it cannot be in your future as well. Perhaps not with this one (Jesse) but with another that is kind and who will love you the way you want to be loved.

ROY: *If that is so, bring him forth! Then I shall release!*

JERI: I would also like to say that the man sitting in this room may have been those things to you in a past life—but he is now a different man, and to haunt him into eternity, which seems to have been your plan, does nothing but wear and tear on you and creates karma for you. It doesn't make it go away, it doesn't change what happened. I can't promise you the kind of young man that you want but what can be provided is an angelic escort to help you move into the Light where there is guidance.

JESSE: Ask her when and what was my name.

JERI: Do you wish to answer those questions?

ROY: *He was a very stately gentleman. We called him Xavier.*

JERI: What was the time, in earth years?

ROY: About the 1430's.

JERI: And location?

ROY: In Central Europe.

JERI: What would we call that country or place today?

JESSE: Spain?

ROY: Yugoslavia and nearby.

JERI: Now we ask if you wish Jesse to speak with you about anything before you make your decision to go?

ROY: *In actuality, I don't want to hear anything from him. If it is time for me to go, I will go. I am just tired and unloved and unwanted and just very unhappy.*

JERI: We thank you for speaking with us. Would you give us your name now?

ROY: *Angelica Du Pont.* (As we proceeded with the release) *Umm, very interesting, you have provided a young man.*

JERI: Handsome, isn't he? We did not provide, the angels did.

ROY: *Very gentle.*

JESSE: Forgive me, god bless you (very sorrowful).

ROY: *Well, I have the same for you, but I will…it's time to go…I am as tormented as much as you are.*

JERI: We now request that you be released, safely into Divine Light, Angelica, and we wish you well.

ROY: (speaking with strong aggressive tone) *On my deathbed I said, "Why does this man forsake me? Why is beautiful Carmelita not taken care of?"*

JERI: Good evening.

ROY: *Is it?*

JESSE: (deep sigh)

ROY: *This man, this man—he married me when I was seventeen. Yes, he had much money, he had wealth, he had title, Spanish court, very close to King Phillip. He was also a Casanova. I knew this, so did my family but we were matched because of family beliefs and family positions. Do you realize how much torment I went through? Wonderful, he was the greatest lover around, maybe five hundred women I'd say. Many times he locked me in a room in the house and beat me and said, "If you ever go out and play like me, I'll kill you." I was afraid, so I stayed at home, locked in the room. The servants had to put food under the door for me. Do you realize I carry my bruises from you, even a broken leg and a broken arm?*

JESSE: (heavy sigh of emotion)

ROY: *Such cruelty, no one needs to live through. Yes, unfortunately, to get back at you, I used your daughter, like the other ones (entities) did. I also used some of your friends. At times you felt you were crazy, when you were under some kind of stuff (marijuana/alcohol) that makes you different, I joined in to make you more crazy.*

JERI: I would like to ask you if you have heard of the concept that on a soul level, we each choose our own path as we are incarnated into a given lifetime?

ROY: *It has been spoken of in my time.*

JERI: Have you thought of why you might have chosen that experience for yourself?

ROY: *I often wondered, and cried about it. Unfortunately, one night, while he was out playing, I could not stand it any more. When they brought my food I cracked the plate and slit my wrists and my throat.*

JERI: Usually, when we choose to go through such a relationship, it has to do with something from our past—in your case, a past karmic situation where you were abusive. Is this possible in your thinking?

ROY: *That is a thought that is new…but as you speak, it shows me pictures.*

JERI: O.K., and did you observe the other woman being released into the Light earlier?

ROY: *Yes.*

JERI: Do you understand what that means?

ROY: I do, as long as I can be as beautiful as when he first met me.

JESSE: (very emotional) I loved you the most!

ROY: *The love was not shown the way I would like to have received it. In the beginning it was wonderful, like a storybook. If you will one day find my diary, everything is in there.*

JESSE: What was my name?

ROY: *You were known as don Jose Espinada. You were a Duke. You also had several other titles because of my family and your own. If you feel ready, perhaps one day you will go to Spain and you will find out.*

JERI: Could you tell us the area of Spain, as we might call it today?

ROY: Predominately Madrid and the Castillian area.

JESSE: When I play the music do you hear it?

ROY: *I hear it. Many times before, you played beautiful music for me. When we first met you always brought wonderful smelling roses to me. One night I came into my room and the entire room was full of red roses and you had me sleep on beautiful smelling rose petals. It was the most cherished evening that is always in my memory. I wish it would have gone on, but it did not.*

JESSE: I can see it

ROY: *Yes, you were a great lover to many, as well as to me. Perhaps I was selfish and perhaps that is why you beat me and did what you did. But now I understand. I must forgive you and forgive myself, so I can move on without the pain.*

JERI: If you are prepared to do this now, we call upon escorts from Archangel Michael to come and assist you…

JESSE: Via con Dios.

ROY: *Via con Dios. They (the guides) have just given me a white rose and now I leave it in front of you. You may not see it, touch it or smell it—but it is a way for me to say I love you and thank you. We are released. He is a beautiful man yet, and I carry love in my heart for him—I go now.*

JERI: To come and assist you safely into Divine Light, and…

ROY: *Tomasio! Tomasio! why did you do it to me?*

JESSE: Ayee! (heavy sigh)

NOTE: By this time we were all a bit wrenched. I thought Jesse was going to lose it. He had been weeping as the tales were told. I had to complete the release…

JERI: And we wish you well Carmelita…(on to the next entity). Good evening, would you give us your name please?

ROY: *It's Anna Marie. Tomasio was wonderful to me. Now I see there were two others that have stayed. I stayed because of the deep love. Yes, you may have beaten me and you may have forsaken me, yet I had my lovers, as you had. My lovers were to replace your love. Every time we kissed or bonded, I saw you, only you—and that is how I lived. On my deathbed, I said I want to follow you and be with you.*

JESSE: Tell me your name.

JERI: She gave it, Anna Marie.

ROY: *Perhaps you do not remember—you gave me a beautiful locket with my name engraved on it. It was the year 1516, the year I met you.*

JESSE: In France?

ROY: *Well, it was partly of France. We traveled much, for you were a soul who needed to travel. You had no homeland really, so I traveled with you, knowing what you did with other women. We are equally at fault, if there is fault—for there is deep love there.*

JESSE: Do you remember the dagger?

ROY: *Yes, though I do not want to…and now I will go. There is a beautiful river of Light here. I will join the others and my family.*

JESSE: Bon soir (crying).

JERI: We call upon escorts from Archangel Michael to come and assist you now, safely into Divine Light and we wish you well, Anna Marie.

ROY: *My name is Beatrice—I am three years old.*

JERI: good evening Beatrice. How old was Jesse when you connected to him?

ROY: *He was three.*

JERI: Are you aware you no longer have your own physical body?

ROY: *I am very aware.*

JERI: Would you share with us what happened that caused you to decease your physical body?

ROY: *Well, my parents did not love me when I was born. They did not take very good care. I would freeze during the winter and I would be exhausted from sunlight during summer. One day, I just gave up, for I was not fed for two days.*

JERI: And so, Jesse was a playmate for you when he was younger?

ROY: *Yes.*

JERI: Have you been watching as the others were released earlier?

ROY: *Those ladies scared me!*

JERI: Yes, I'll bet they did, and you've had to hide from them, haven't you?

ROY: *Yes.*

JERI: Would you like to be released also?

ROY: *Yes.*

JERI: OK.

JESSE: You can go now, it's O.K.

ROY: *Thank you.*

JERI: We now call upon escorts from Archangel Michael to come and assist you, Beatrice, safely into Divine Light and we wish you well.

JESSE: (crying) It is safe where you're going, it's pretty there.

ROY: *I can see the other children there.*

JESSE: You'll meet my friend, Paul. This one just needed protection—she'll have it now.

ROY: *There's a motorcycle guy, he says, Hey dude!*

JESSE: Uh oh! He's there? I know these folks.

JERI: Good evening. What is your name?

ROY: *The name's Butch. You been kicked around, kicked in your butt, slugged in your stomach, slapped on the head by me several times.*

JESSE: That's it!

ROY: *And you've been boozing and you've been doing all kinds of things in the past—but you and me have had a lot of good times together.*

JERI: How old was Jesse when you connected to him?

ROY: *I saw him at about eight, but I had other duties. Came back when he was fifteen, kinda hung around a little while.*

JESSE: Yeah!

ROY: *Then I left—then came back about seventeen. It's been off and on since then. I haven't been around all the time.*

JESSE: Good fun riding, aay?

ROY: *Oh yeah!*

JERI: Did you know Jesse before your death?

JESSE: Way back.

ROY: *Yep! And it's time to go now.*

JESSE: Hey man, there's a better ride waitin.

ROY: *Hey, yeah, there's a Harley here waiting for me.*

JESSE: That one no need gas already, go.

JERI: It's brand new and there's not a mark on it.

ROY: *Sure is.*

JESSE: No leaks, good tires…going.

ROY: *Good tires, chrome fenders.*

JESSE: Good, go.

ROY: *I'm going.*

JERI: Is there anyone else with you?

ROY: *Oh, there's this beautiful chick name Jane. She's been around with me, bouncing back and forth to different people, and in his (Jesse's) dreams, if he remembers—he's had some three-way sessions with us.*

JESSE: Uh oh!

ROY: *It's been fun.*

JERI: I would also like to ask Jane if she wishes to be released?

JESSE: Yeah, go for it—and the rest of the friends too, that we used to ride with. Go, go also—it's in the memory banks. Don't play here, there's a better ride waitin'.

ROY: There are about seventeen motorcycles right now.

JESSE: A bunch of em, there's a bunch.

JERI: We ask for all the discarnates connected to Butch, riding with Butch, to gather now.

ROY: *Hey man, ya know there's about three hundred of us right now?*

JESSE: There's a bunch…and you remember last year, out by Sprecklesville, and I was riding by myself, goin' out to Nathan's house?

ROY: *Yeah?*

JESSE: And you guys came up behind me. I said O.K., let's ride then, and we rode. You all had a good time and I said afterwards, thank you very much. And you picked me up again, a couple nights later in the same area. I said O.K. you wanna ride with me? Let's go. When the ride's over, it's time for you to go. Follow your own lights. And now's the time to do that—and thanks for the company, I needed it that night. It's time for you to get out there and get some real ridin done where you won't have to go through any stop signs—and nobody's gonna be chasin' you. Just go and enjoy it. It's the ride you been waitin' for, that you couldn't find up that lonely road that you were goin' on. Now's the time.

ROY: *Hey, man, thanks a lot. I just sent about seventy-five ahead, no problem. We'll see ya later.*

JERI: We now request an escort from Archangel Michael to come and assist each and every one of you, safely into Divine Light and we wish you a great ride.

ROY: *The last guy says, Happy hog heaven.*

JESSE: Go for it, and thanks for the safety tips.

JERI: It's a little noisy at the "gates" this evening, isn't it?

ROY: I don't know where this white dog came in, or if it was a pet, but it's like a little puppy…kind of staring at you (Jesse) and licking your foot, saying goodbye. Oh, it just ran after the bikers.

JERI: We ask that all animals be included in this release. Are there any other attachments?

ROY: Only a little year and a half old baby that Jesse's daughter was holding on to. The baby is being released by the angels.

And so it was. Jesse had remembered numerous dreams where he had seen certain things—and people we encountered in this session. This helped to put the pieces together. His life situation greatly improved and his daughter's situation leveled off. Of course, each person is still left with their own personal issues to work on—but it is so much easier without outside interference.

The following case would probably make a good movie script. It shows how karmic attachments can accumulate, lifetime after lifetime, compounding the

negative influences which can create great turmoil and discomfort at a very personal level.

CASE 7: The client is Rebecca is a woman in her late forties. Her childhood
was very bleak and she has a long history of unsuccessful relationships, psychosis
and alcoholism. This theme runs all through her family from her childhood and
on through her own children's childhood. They are adults now. She said there
was verbal and physical abuse and no love in her childhood, which continued
into her marriage of many years, to the present time.

Shortly before the clearing, a counselor suggested to Rebecca that she had
been abused as a child, through satanic ritual, by one of her caretakers who was
described as a German woman. There was no material lack as the family had a
great deal of wealth through the father.

As we move into the clearing process, the scenario unfolds and all the pieces
come together of a life-long puzzle that actually spans generations. There is also a
startling discovery regarding the true identity of Rebecca's father. We will also be
dealing with an astral scenario with several players. The channels are Roy and
Suzanne.

IN SESSION: Rebecca specifically wants to uncover and release any blockages
from childhood that may be hindering her in having positive relationships.

SUZ: I'm seeing a doorway but there's nobody there—the door is open.

JERI: I call forward a doorkeeper or dweller, if there is one.

ROY: I'm hearing a voice and it has an accent.

JERI: O.K., hello.

REBECCA: (very strong voice) *Ya! Das is me! Das is Anna!* (German accent)

JERI: Good evening—what is your relationship to Rebecca?

REBECCA: *Ya! She's da kinder! She's da kinder! Ya, she's the one!*

JERI: She is the child?

REBECCA: *Ya! She's da kinder!*

JERI: But what child? Who's child are you speaking of? Roy, do you see a dicar-
nate?

ROY: There is a heavy presence. She's about 230 pounds, dark brown hair
streaked with blonde.

JERI: OK, we're going to transfer her to Roy, simply because, as a channel he can
filter energy so we can expedite with focused communication. I now request of
Anna to speak through Roy. How old are you?

ROY: She says she is thirty-four.

JERI: Are you aware that you no longer have your own physical body?

ROY: Yes, she has been with Rebecca's aunt and her nurse.

JERI: What is your connection to Rebecca?

ROY: She is protecting her (Rebecca). She has never had love or protection.

JERI: Are you connected to the aunt and Rebecca?

ROY: Both, since childhood.

JERI: Do you go back and forth?

ROY: Yes, she doesn't understand why the aunt has never taken charge of Rebecca and helped her.

JERI: When Rebecca questioned her aunt recently, about her childhood, are you saying she did not tell her the whole truth?

ROY: *Ya, ya, ya!*

JERI: Would you care to share the information with us, since you were there in Rebecca's childhood, albeit as a discarnate.

ROY: Besides Rebecca being abused, other kids in the family were also.

JERI: Are those the cousins who lived downstairs?

ROY: Yes

JERI: Abused by whom?

ROY: Verbally and sometimes physically. She says there was no love in the family. It was a situation of "marriage and family" as a duty to conform.

JERI: Why are you attached to the aunt (on father's side)?

ROY: She was the only one who took care of everybody.

REBECCA: Everyone took turns trying to help care for thirteen of us cousins. I was an only child. Three aunts had no children and they would take turns.

JERI: What year did you die, Anna?

ROY: *1904*

JERI: Could you answer some questions about Rebecca's childhood?

ROY: *Yes*

JERI: There is a counselor who seems to think Rebecca was exposed to a German caretaker who involved her in some kind of satanic ritual. What do you know of that?

ROY: *No, no, minister did that. My family, before, in Germany, we belonged to a religious group who was not Christian—they believe the old way.*

JERI: What do you know about a possible family curse?

ROY: She is taking a deep breath and screaming. *Three generations ago, one of the uncles was in charge of a cult. He was the witch and they had a church of earthly things* (nature-based religious sect) *and connected to spirit through the trees and animals. They could do many things of manifestation, out of the air.*

JERI: Where is the uncle now?

ROY: *Dead, but running around in the family, driving everybody crazy—that's why I protect Rebecca.*

JERI: Has Rebecca ever been exposed to a situation…?

ROY: *No, no, no!*

JERI: I was going to say, such as a nightmare of these old activities of ritual?

ROY: *Yes, this man is affecting everybody!*

JERI: He is still enacting those rituals, still playing his role but he is just doing it in the astral.

ROY: Rebecca and other family members on father's side have inherited the power and the karma.

JERI: What is this uncle's name?

ROY: *Herr Doctor Steinw_____?* (Not clear on tape)

JERI: I call him forward now. Would you give us your first name please?

ROY: He is standing away, behind a tree with a torch.

JERI: We request any violent entities be placed into containment, now. I call you (uncle) forward for the purpose of communication.

ROY: He is speaking in German but it is coming in translation: *Why are you disturbing me! Why are you interfering in my family affairs? Those who have killed me have set this curse against my family. They took away everything we owned at that time and persecuted the family. Those of the various Christian Churches spoke out against my family and created these energies of harm towards the family.*

There were three other practitioners present who were just as powerful as the uncle was and happy about what had happened to him. They had set a curse in motion against the family so they could never grow to the strength of what the uncle had attained. Through the centuries, none of the progenitors would have the power, and whenever they might try to seek companions, these will be loveless companionships. This curse will go on, until broken, if ever.

The uncle is saying he has done a lot in the ethers (astral) to get back at the other three, for they are in the astral as well. He also wants to get at Rebecca because he feels she can help him. He says, *"This confounded "butch" (Anna) keeps blocking my way. I can't do anything."*

JERI: Rebecca is a channel. That's why he wants to get into her.

REBECCA: I had an uncle Will, I just got a chill about him, that he's also involved and he's a doctor, Doctor Willy.

JERI: This uncle (discarnate) is incredibly powerful, but he is also in fierce judgement about everyone. He trusts noone, he is very angry and bitter. At this time, I ask you (uncle) and Anna to stand by, as I now call forward the source, the makers of the curse.

ROY: The three men appeared—they are screaming and want to know why they are contained and why we are within their realm.

JERI: Because we have been asked to assist—and perhaps it is time this situation be finished…

ROY: *But we are only doing what he did to us when we killed him.* Evidently he put a curse on them, originally.

JERI: These energies are affecting people who don't know any of you. They know nothing of the situation.

ROY: Two of them are saying that he made them so mad that they threw the curse back at him, "for all eternity."

JERI: I now ask all of you in both factions—would you be willing to end this situation in order to release your families and yourselves?

ROY: Two of them are saying, *"If he will undo what he did to us, we will undo what we did to him and his family, but can we reverse history?"*

JERI: No one can change what happened in the past, but I suggest, with your abilities, your powers and perhaps even your "connections", that you look even farther into the past and see the truth of where all of this started. Going back into past lives beyond your present knowing. Each of you, lifetime after lifetime, back and forth, perpetrators becoming victims, victims becoming perpetrators, on and on…

It is time to stop—so that on a soul/spirit level, everyone can be released and move out of this continuous siege of darkness. How many centuries do you need to be vengeful? Rebecca is here to request that you be disconnected from herself and her family, through Ho'oponopono. It is her right by Divine Law. What is left is for each of you to decide if you wish to remain in containment or join in the process of release. We ask you now. Uncle first…

ROY: He has calmed considerably and just wants to protect his family and to make correction.

JERI: And the three men?

ROY: They are screaming, *that's all we've been trying to do, is protect our families and ourselves as well.*

JERI: Alright then, with your agreement, we will proceed with Ho'oponopono between all of you.

ROY: They are all kind of shocked because when you said Ho'oponopono, Hawaiian warriors appeared behind them. They are rather scared, but they agree.

JERI: Whatever works, we will proceed. On behalf of this entire family lineage, we now invoke the entire Ho'oponopono process between each one of you. We request that all disharmonious energies between you, now be transmuted into pure Light. As a completion—do each one of you ask for and give in return, for-giveness, for anything that may have ever been said or done to cause harm. Make your statement now (all made their statements). Then, so be it. We now request Divine blessing for each person involved, and Divine Guidance, leading you onto the path of your highest purpose.

ROY: They are all asking now, *can all of our discarnate families leave this darkness?*
JERI: Yes, of course, this is what we are talking about. We ask that you gather together as we call upon escorts from Archangel Michael, to come and assist each of you, safely into Divine Light and we thank you for speaking with us, and we wish you well.

ROY: Anna turned to Rebecca and is saying, *See, I told you, you were the one, you were the one.* She is kissing and hugging you, Rebecca. She will go now, along with her seven sisters who are with her, and have also been running amok in the family. They came with your father, she is saying, he was born in Germany and the whole family has had one awful experience after another, terrible, terrible things.

As soon as one married into the family, they automatically took on the curse. You (Rebecca) and seven other cousins have been the main targets.

REBECCA: One of my girl cousins died a terrible death from alcoholism. The youngest daughter just now died at forty-two and her son was always very emo-tionally disturbed. They all seem to have very severe problems.

JERI: This curse was very powerful. It was a triangulation energy (the power of three), the most intense for manifestation.

The minister was seeing a real picture and where there is smoke there is fire. He assumed it was present-life, physical reality. He may not even be open to the concept of reincarnation or the fact that discarnates can have an effect on those in body. This creates great limitation for solution of such issues. The minister men-tions an uncle. We find him to be an ancestor who is very much part of your fam-ily situation (albeit deceased).

REBECCA: Another practitioner also said he felt my father is not my real father. Is that connected to the curse?

ROY: The picture I have of your father is bald, heavy-set, very prosperous. He is saying now, "Tell her I love her."

REBECCA: Last year, during a regression, my father (deceased) came and said he was not my father, he was a homosexual. I just don't know.

ROY: He wasn't your real father, your mother had a lover on the side.

REBECCA: That is something…so I don't know my father?

ROY: He knows you, he is deceased now and he is here. All he says is that he loves you.

REBECCA: The German family I grew up in then…was not my family? Yet the curse was on me too? I have his name!

JERI: You were included.

REBECCA: It's hard to understand how my mother (now deceased) could have a lover, although, she was very strange, very beautiful, a devout Catholic.

JERI: Others knew but kept it quiet, and as long as that continued, it was fine. Some actually sympathized with her.

REBECCA: My father was fifty-five when I was born, my mother was thirty-five. He was very dictatorial, extremely wealthy. The whole family worked in his business.

JERI: He was doing what was expected by marrying, and your mother wanted the life of luxury and didn't care if he was homosexual. She did not really plan to have children.

REBECCA: I was even wondering if she was trying to miscarry me when I was born three months early. There was a lot of mystery around the story she tells.

JERI: We ask Divine Guidance to share any other information regarding that situation.

ROY: What they are showing is that there was a lot of fighting between your legal father and mother. He beat her as well. She even tried sleeping pills at one point and she also drank a lot.

REBECCA : Yes she did, she was an alcoholic.

ROY: And, she wanted to kill you.

JERI: As we began to release the legal father and any others attached…the mother came through Rebecca in a drunken rage, spewing vile, belittling statements at Rebecca. We placed her in containment and called Angelic assistants to calm her. We proceeded to cut cords from her. As the mother started to speak, I saw a whole crowd attached to her. They have probably been there since her youth.

SUZ: As soon as she started speaking through her, I got a wave of a crowd sitting next to me (Suz is sitting next to Rebecca)

JERI: Your mother is the schizophrenic, Rebecca.

SUZ: At least, if not MPD (Multiple Personality Disorder).

ROY: That was the OTHER that your husband…

NOTE: (Rebecca's mother came screaming through her at this time)

ROY:…And your boyfriend were dealing with.

REBECCA: *These are all a bunch of incompetents, that's what they all are, including you...*(Rebecca began to cry)

JERI: We call upon escorts from Archangel Michael to come now...and release you and all that is connected to you, safely into Divine Light and we wish you well. For those who wish to participate in a Ho'oponopono process, we will begin now...and are they all leaving or are some hanging on?

ROY: (chuckling) they're fighting, but they are leaving.

SUZ: Some are, but as you complete the process they will go. I suggest the sooner the better. It feels like it's getting more crowded in here.

REBECCA: (laughing) it's the funniest thing.

JERI: (we completed Ho'oponopono and release with mother and others) Is she going peacefully?

ROY: She was kicking and screaming, but is calming now. She just wants to get away from Rebecca.

SUZ: She even thinks the angels are incompetent!

REBECCA: (laughing, releasing tension)

ROY: She is on her way—big surprise. Rebecca, what's your legal father's name?

REBECCA: Andrew Martin

JERI: Is he present?

ROY: He is just saying he is sorry he wasn't kind to you. Is there another Andrew?

REBECCA: Uncle Andrew who was the one who washed my mouth out!

ROY: He was your father.

REBECCA: That's my mother's brother! He's the one who lived downstairs.

ROY: Your legal father promised him he would take care of you, knowing you were his child.

JERI: No wonder your mother drank!

REBECCA: Oh my gosh! I'm getting chills! Because when I was talking to a friend about this the other day—I said that when I was a child, I thought he was my father and my cousins were my sisters.

JERI: On a psychic level, as a child, you knew that.

REBECCA: Yes, and he was always picking at me and correcting me, always.

ROY: He felt very guilty.

REBECCA: So this is why, my cousin...I hated her so much my whole life because she's really my sister.

JERI: And you were jealous of how he treated her, you didn't understand consciously. We are both your daughters, why do you treat her better than me? Is that how you felt?

REBECCA: Yes. We always played together.

JERI: The other practitioners were right in what they saw, they just didn't have the story straight. There are two major issues here. One is the heavy curse with ancient Pagan ancestors, seemingly satanic, and an uncle. Your uncle was your father!

ROY: Interesting—yes, and they're both here.

JERI: Do either one of you wish to say anything else at this time?

ROY: The legal father is just crying and saying, "I'm sorry." He wanted to make a show of his life but never treated anyone right. Your blood father is also crying and saying he's sorry too, but he truly loves you, and his guilt drove him to be abusive.

JERI: In fear of discovery…

SUZ:…If someone noticed that he did love you as a daughter…

JERI:…And then to live with the shame and humiliation…

REBECCA:…And one of seven children in a Catholic family, with sister and brother sleeping together…

ROY: He says they always loved each other (mother and blood father) and they experimented in their teens. She stopped it then. Later when she was drunk, he seduced her.

REBECCA: I wonder if my blood father's wife knew?

JERI: Have you each completed your speaking?

ROY: Yes, and they ask for forgiveness.

JERI: (we completed the Ho'oponopono process)

ROY: Your legal father is saying, *I wish I could have given you "the golden ring" that you really deserve.*

REBECCA: God! I always used to say that as a child! I wanted "the golden ring!"

JERI: And so are each of you ready to be released?

ROY: They are.

JERI: We call upon escorts from Archangel Michael to come and assist each of you, safely into Divine Light and we wish you well. We give thanks to our personal Divine Guidance and we give thanks to Archangel Michael and all other Divine beings who have assisted us this evening—it is complete.

This case was a good example of a practitioner (the counselor) who is not clarifying his information. May I encourage anyone to acknowledge the influence of other-dimensional beings when working with your clients. This understanding could prevent the issue of misplaced blame for abuse that is often put upon innocent parents or others. This is a tragedy, which has devastated the lives of many families.

This case also shows how far-reaching the Ho'oponopono process can be to clear ancestral disharmony and curses from present generations. Those cultures who practice ancestor worship, as I have mentioned elsewhere, know what they are dealing with in the world of spirit, the world of those who have gone before us. They are not always gone!

The main difference between the living, if you will, and the deceased, is the simple fact that the latter have no physical for us to SEE!

In many cases the accounts of certain scenarios or the birth and death records are available to trace for verification. Some discarnates we encounter are in the files of unsolved homicides.

Others we have released were from airplane disasters, drownings, auto accidents and more. One discarnate asked us immediately, "What year is it?" When we told him, he was in shock! He knew then that he had been killed in an explosion involving nuclear energy, but it had happened in the future!

Possession And Crime

○ ○

In memory of my grandfather, Detective Lieutenant Le Roy Sanderson
Homicide, Los Angeles Police Department

It is my experience that possession is very much a part of criminal behavior, to a greater or lesser degree, or in combination with specific biological and emotional dysfunction of the host. These dysfunctions make a person more susceptible to possession. It seems to be a vicious circle. All are connected, holistically speaking.

I will address the crime of homicide, citing specific situations as I relate them to possession and the strong influence this has as a factor as the main catalyst for the behavior. The cases that involve multiple personality disorder (MPD) or schizophrenia are the most severe, especially with killers that are considered to be sociopaths. Although some kill just one or two victims, I will focus mostly on the issue of serial killing.

Is It Really Satan?

I would like to touch on the subject of satanic or other ritual abuse. We have had a couple of clearing cases in this category and I would say that this type of possession is always involves a group entity. Sacrificial killings and cannibalism are frequently committed although the bodies are not often found. There are more groups than most people realize, but no one wants to believe it because of the fear involved. The activities, the control and the manipulation within many of these cults is frightening and very far reaching, in the present and from ancient times.

These groups are usually generational, as are the entities attached. Some of them are dark sorcerers of the past, or members of dark secret orders or fraternities from antiquity. We should simply be aware that they exist and perhaps do a little research for our education. Today they are sometimes masked as a church and you will often find this type of activity connected to drug abuse, prostitution and child pornography on an international scale.

A Murder

In his book, *Exorcism*, author Eugene Maurey tells of a murder committed by a person with Multiple Personality Disorder. Paul Miskomen beat his wife to death in 1979. Paul was diagnosed as MPD by Dr. Ralph Allison. California Superior Court Judge, Sheldon Grossfield declared Miskomen not guilty by reason of insanity, and ordered him to be placed in a state mental hospital—released after fourteen months.

The "personality" (discarnate) who actually murdered Miskomen's wife willingly admitted his dislike for her, his guilt for her death, and his name, Jack Kelly. This information was disclosed during an examination by psychiatrists using truth serum and hypnosis.

Maurey states that Dr. Allison, author of the book *Minds in Many Pieces*, believed Kelly to be an attached spirit who was manipulating Miskomen. I agree completely although I don't agree with the court's verdict of insanity. Possession often feels like insanity and looks like insanity, but it is possession and needs to be acknowledged and treated accordingly.

The doctor did not want to deal with rejection and ridicule, so he did not state his diagnosis in court! I don't blame him. At some point, hopefully sooner than later, the professionals involved must be open to being educated about the reality of possession. Maurey tells of many situations where he has done clearings (exorcism) directly or from a distance (absentee) on those who were manifesting criminal behavior.

Postpartum Homicide?

This is a tragic situation, which later received more attention. In *From Cradle to Grave*, author Joyce Egginton writes of an accused child killer. "Marybeth Tinning seems to have two personalities and has displayed markedly alternating attitudes about her nine dead children."

Others who knew her or encountered her through the years prior to her arrest, described her temper as evil and terrifying, especially the look in her eyes. I feel this case is discarnate possession. A look at postpartum psychosis can show the similarities in symptoms. Egginton refers to a study of this psychosis.

Dr. Stuart S. Asch, professor of clinical psychiatry at New York Hospital-Cornell Medical Center, has made a study of postpartum psychosis (depression). He states, "It's a form of suicide" which can be triggered by a traumatic family crisis. This could be the death of a parent during pregnancy or some other trauma or even a preexisting trauma manifesting as depression (there is a great deal of buried anger involved with depression). The mother may have felt unloved or unwanted and she may have been abused in childhood...she may transfer her anger to the baby and kill it...she may be unaware of reality, but deep inside she knows what she is doing.

After birth, there is an inner jealousy of the baby and the attention it is usually given by all the others involved further intensifies the mother's memories of her childhood rejection or other traumas. Although, during pregnancy, the mother gets lots of care and attention—after birth, it is transferred to the baby! Other dysfunctional psychological scenarios or delusions can accompany this pattern, each one unique to the mother's individual psyche or that of a discarnate in attachment!

Discarnate attachment follows the "like attracts like" rule and they can exacerbate already existing negative feelings. I feel some discarnates are picked up at the hospital when she goes into labor (becomes vulnerable physically and emotionally) and gives birth.

Another situation of discarnate attachment often occurs early in childhood, due to the abused condition, endured by the mother as a child (already mentioned). The discarnate usually stays with the person through the years, often as a companion or secret playmate or guardian. When the host grows up and has a baby, the discarnate can become jealous and enraged and retaliate.

Manipulation of a host is easier when the host is in a weakened state, such as that of a mother recovering from the birth process. If this type of mother is actually schizophrenic or has MPD, I would guarantee possession is involved. I feel the case of Marybeth Tinning is a classic example.

Egginton describes in her writing that these mothers have a lot of trouble keeping their stories clear. They cannot tell you the whole truth, will not admit to all they did. I suggest it is because they are not acting alone and don't really remember what they did because the discarnate was in control. It is common for the host to have memory lapse at those times.

Egginton relates that often the mother stops the killing act, rushes the baby to the hospital for help—only to re-attempt the killing at a later time. Perhaps the mother is trying to save the baby from the discarnate, because she didn't start the killing in the first place! May I suggest some simple inquiry into these possibilities to avoid more tragic deaths?

Serial Killers

I believe there is intense and expansive possession involved in situations involving serial killers. These cases are bizarre in the realm of human behavior due to the extreme nature of the violence.

Some of the killers act like split personalities—others display symptoms of multiple personality disorder. Most are sociopaths (having no conscience), while others display all of the above. And there seems to be an increase in numbers of serial killers in the U.S., while there are few, if any cases from other countries. Perhaps these cases in the U.S. are just over-exposed by the media.

The main ingredient that I find to be very other-worldly is the ghoulish nature of some of the killers. It is the very same thing that seems to be so fascinating to the community at large. There are books, trading cards, T-shirts and weird fan clubs for some of these killers. Perhaps it is just the fascination with the dark part of ourselves, the part that is usually controlled, and our compulsion to know and understand the cause or source of what appears to be evil incarnate.

In our clearing work, we have not knowingly done a clearing on a serial killer client, although we have encountered two known killers (executed) and released them from a client who was in restraints in the mental health unit of our local hospital. He was out of control, and had to be restrained, to be brought in.

I have discussed the possibility, with my partner, of doing an "absentee" session on a known serial killer who is in prison, with the client's consent, of course. I feel it would be important research and I would encourage the assistance of medical personnel.

In our practice we never solicit our clients. All of our clients are referred by practitioners of various healing arts, other psychics or other clients. In any case, I do feel strongly about the high probability of severe possession involvement (with) regarding serial killers and would like to extend our services into this area of research. I will share some information on this subject and ask you to evaluate it for yourself.

Who and Why?

In the book, *Serial Killers*, Joel Norris makes a list of conditions, during childhood, that serial killers all have in common. These include: parental abuse, violence, brain injuries resulting from physical trauma, neglect, chronic malnutrition, childhood cognitive disabilities, chronic alcohol and drug abuse, inherited neurological disorder and toxic environment. This is enough to make anyone severely dysfunctional, at least. But what tips some over the edge, into murder? Unfortunately, these childhood conditions are rampant in this country and produce many criminals, yet in comparison only a limited few become serial killers.

Perhaps what makes the difference is the presence of "attached discarnates" who are equally or more dysfunctional than their host. What you have then is a couple or a group of entities resulting in an intensification of the shared negative traits, keeping in mind that like attracts like. It can also be a situation of a weakened but very angry person with a very dominant and violent discarnate inciting the acting out, or actually doing the act, using the host as a puppet.

In either case, the discarnate is the catalyst for the violence. As I have read many accounts of serial killers, I continue to see that the classic patterns for attachment are there in most cases and present in severe proportions.

Norris states in his book, "Our evaluations of serial killers show that each of them has an amalgamation of symptoms that point to a type of disease (dis-ease) that can actually shape their behavior patterns."

I feel it is the other way around. The environmental behavior patterns of their youth have shaped their disease. Their dis-ease, if you will, is the result of sharing their body with a malevolent spirit! The host's emotional traumas are so intense and predominant, that they become wide open for attachment, increasing the fragmentation between their mind/body/spirit. As one or more spirits move in to feed on these strong negative emotions, the host has less and less control and becomes more reactive to their (discarnate's) intensified emotional disorder, creating severe imbalance within and without.

The intensity of negative emotional patterns increases with each discarnate that attaches. It is similar to a shark. If one feeds on a fresh kill, others will be attracted to the "scent" and the feeding vibration—then others and eventually, there is a frenzy of multiple sharks feeding on one carcass, some nibbling, others gorging! The dominant animal feeds the most aggressively.

Similarly, in full possession "feeding," the dominant discarnate presides—the strongest has most control. It is the natural order of nature. The movie, Lord of the Flies, tells it quite well. In "common" possession/attachment, the host is the dominant person and presides and the discarnate has less influence.

The very nature of the type of spirits that are catalysts for violent behavior is destructive and murderous. Some have the ability to kill their host as well as others. These are powerful spirits or groups of them. Keep in mind they can come from any culture and any time period from the past where killing for war, human sacrifice, or merely on a whim, was normal. These activities are very wrong in our society, but not in theirs.

But They Seem Normal

Norris tells of further observations of serial killers. They can seem "normal" in appearance and behavior. Often their victims are missing for months, years, or are never found. They seem fascinated with the whole killing process, especially the, "…remains of their crime. They visit the graves of their victims and attend their funerals."

They monitor the investigations of their crimes and often communicate with those involved as if it were all a game. When they have exhausted their supply of preferred prey (depending on their personal dysfunctional reality) and have not been caught, they move to another town, to continue their activities.

"Killing his victims at the rate of two or more a month, year after year and often for decades, the serial murderer commits his crimes in numbers vastly disproportionate to those of the traditional murderer." Norris states that it is becoming an epidemic, and is due to an increase of child abuse, chronic malnutrition, drug abuse and alcoholism passed from generation to generation. I totally agree. The healthy environment of a "loving family life" has deteriorated drastically in the last fifty years. I have witnessed it myself; I am fifty nine at this writing.

Addicted or Possessed?

Norris writes, "The serial murderer, unlike the traditional criminal, is addicted to his passion…he is his ultimate victim…He may loathe what he does and despise his own weakness, but he can do nothing on his own to control it." This is the very nature of possession. First, most people do not know what they are dealing with, or whom. Second, no one else knows either, including any social, medical, police or church professionals they might encounter.

To continue with Norris's observations, "Perversely, he wishes for death, and the threat of the gas chamber, the electric chair, or lethal injection is only an inducement to keep committing murders until he is caught and put to death…This is why, upon apprehension, so many serial killers readily confess to their crimes and beg for punishment."

This behavior continues to be conducive of possession, for a couple of reasons. One, the killer host is dreadfully aware that someone or something else is in control and he is horrified as he witnesses the carnage, and feels the only escape from the nightmare is incarceration or his own death. Some feel they are cursed and, indeed, they very well could be. Another modality is that the discarnate(s) wants the death of the host, as it will be even easier to control him on the other side, as a slave spirit. Together they can hop onto another host and continue the energy feeding and even the killing.

I feel that Jeffrey Dahmer was possessed by several spirits, and is now, very possibly, attached (in group) to one or all of the men who killed him in prison. It is just a theory, but it is common behavior for vengeful discarnates. It can be easily ascertained.

Norris writes, "Most serial killers are only partially aware of what they are doing, and because they have reduced their victims to totemic objects their recollections of the actual murders are very sketchy and vague." It is common with full possession, as in Multiple Personality Disorder that the host does not remember many of his own actions. May I suggest, it is because they are not in control. Their own consciousness is forced to the side, literally.

It is no different than stage-show hypnosis, where the volunteer has no memory of barking like a dog. In possession someone (or many) is sharing your mind! Any one can control the "spotlight" at a given time. The dominant one is in charge when it wants to be. It is the same behavioral scenario as in a social group of those in physical bodies. We all know people who are like that. The only difference is that we can leave their presence, a host cannot. A host can withdraw mentally, emotionally, or commit suicide, but only if the "dominant" will allow it!

This is usually the case because the host does not realize he is possessed, or does not know how to free him/her self of entities. Often when the killer is caught and questioned, the discarnate will manifest in some way, as in schizophrenia, or the discarnate will become silent and the host is left to deal with the situation in bewilderment, fear and remorse.

Carlton Gary was convicted in 1980 and put on death row in Georgia. He could not remember the actual killings he did. He insisted that he watched, while SOMEONE ELSE committed the crimes! The only surviving victim swore until her later death, that a white man raped and tried to kill her. Gary is black!

Was she seeing the discarnate psychically? I think she was. He even resembled someone she actually knew. This is also possible. Revenge after death through possession of a host one can manipulate.

Altered States of Consciousness

Norris describes seven phases in the serial killer's process. The first is referred to as the Aura Phase: "There is some form of withdrawal from everyday reality that indicates the beginnings of a behavior change. First, time seems to slow down. Sounds and colors become more vivid. Odors become more intense…"

I would describe that as an altered state of consciousness. I believe it occurs when the resident discarnate is moving into control inside the "aura" and the host is then "channeling" a higher vibrational spirit. Which is exactly what a discarnate is! This is very common with normal experiences of psychics channeling when tuning-in for a reading or counseling session. It also occurs in meditation for mind expansion and in hypnosis. As sensitives, we experience this often.

Norris states, "At the very beginning of the Aura Phase, some serial killers can still verbalize their feelings and report that they are losing their grip on reality. The Aura Phase once entered, however, is like a portal between two realities…" Of course it is!

I suggest that Norris is absolutely correct in his observation, his interpretation. The host (serial killer) is being "moved" out of third-dimensional (3-D) reality by the discarnate, put on the side, and the discarnate moves into that space/spotlight of 3-D consciousness, directing the actions of the host, until the killing is over! This is an example of a slave spirit incarnate. The extreme example would be a zombie, except that "control" is remote—from outside the body.

Discarnates can also have hundreds of slave spirits attached to them—whether they are through energy attraction (like attracts like) or gathered to be slave-spirits to dominate. There are practitioners of the Craft (deceased or in body) who are specifically "spirit catchers." They control and manipulate discarnates to do their bidding, often to control or manipulate another.

The other phases as described in Norris's book are, "2: The Trolling Phase, searching for the next victim. 3: The Wooing Phase, disarming their victims in preparation. 4: Capture, the victim is trapped into the situation. 5: The Murder, the high. 6: The Totem Phase, for those who continue ritual with the dead remains, usually to keep the high going longer."

Phase 7 is called "The Depression Phase." Many serial killers report depression after the killing, and "…for days or weeks after the most recent murder the killer will inhabit a shadowy world of gloom in which he feeds on his sorrow…"

May I suggest that being forced to kill someone would create severe depression in any one of us—and as the host appears to feed on his sorrow, I believe the discarnate(s) are the ones enjoying that "meal" of negative energy, a very dreadful parasite. The very act of murder, with or without sexual activity, creates an intense degree of energy that is FOOD, which empowers the negative discarnate.

There is another situation that can increase the sorrow of the host. It is when a victim jumps aboard (the host) as they are deceasing their physical bodies. This can occur if the victim is vengeful at the time of their death, although I feel this is rare.

Capture and Incarceration

Often, when capture of the killer does occur, Norris states, "…be it in prison or a hospital for the criminally insane, a medical treatment facility, or any place where systematic rules govern the daily activities of the inmates, there is a marked improvement in their behavior." May I suggest, the host finally feels safe, possibly for the first time in his life, or because whoever possesses the host, feels safe or is in containment…or they have abandoned the host, literally, jumped off!

Norris continues, "Thriving in this controlled environment and sustained by any improvement in their diets and receiving frequent counseling, the killers become mercurial or placid, bonding closely with male and female authority figures…"

Could this behavior change be due to the substitute for the home and family the host never had? Perhaps an environment that even the discarnate never had. Or that with the tight security of such a facility, the spirits lie dormant, or finally the spirits are gone!

It is also possible that the resident discarnate simply goes into neutral and waits for the death of the host, or waits for a new host. It depends on the situation. There is no time in their dimension and they are quite safe, even if the host is executed. The discarnate is always safe, which could explain the commonly shared but unusual medical/psychological patterns, as told by Norris in the following statement: "One of the most significant…patterns is a failure to perceive punishment as a deterrent to their actions and a fascination with police procedures and the officers who are pursuing them."

I suggest, that if a killer is invisible, he cannot be deterred by any third-dimensional action, which is why there is no fear. It is not they who will be punished—they can vacate the host at will and always find another. I also believe that many of these types of discarnates are "sociopaths," basically, they are dead criminals in attachment/possession to live criminals. Research into this issue would be very informative. Very often, the discarnates attached to our clients fear us, the exorcists, for obvious reasons, which is why we activate containment at the time of the first call.

One can also see how an invisible killer could become quite fascinated by those police and procedures that are working to stop them and even interact with them, simply because they can, without detection. There is a definite empowerment the discarnate must feel from this perspective. They have the freedom to do what they want, when they want, without consequence. This can and must be changed.

Eventually, Norris writes, "...they tend to lose their sense of the past and to confuse the events of their lives. It is almost as if the murders never took place, as if part of their consciousness has been shut down, and they begin to function like other institutionalized patients who rely on their external environments for all sentient activity. And almost all of them are markedly without remorse, as if the moral responsibility for the crimes they committed has been borne by someone else..."

In a case of full possession, the host would easily lose their sense of the past, especially since they were not fully present at that time, not in full consciousness. The host did not really intend to do the murders and they know, albeit subconsciously, that someone else is responsible. If the discarnate leaves the host do the memories of the discarnate's deeds go with them? Yes. Does the host retain all of those memories as well? Yes, although buried deeply in the subconscious. These memories can be accessed via hypnosis.

As the abused, neglected or controlled children that hosts still are, due to severe emotional atrophy (common with alcoholism or substance abuse), would normally rely on the external environment for all sentient activity and would want to bond with and try to please and seek approval from the "surrogate parents," represented by the institutional staff and/or other officials.

As time passes, "...when the appropriate feelings of remorse return, the grief and sadness have more to do with the tragedies of their own lives than with the lives of their victims." If I may suggest, this is because the victims were not theirs to begin with. However, these feelings originated in their own painful childhood, and these traumas must be processed for their healing. I would first recommend a clearing.

I would suspect the discarnates in these cases are also dealing with abusive backgrounds and similar profiles as the hosts. An example of this is found in Norris's book in the story of convicted killer, Gary Schaefer. "His sister Dorothy has conclusively refuted any accusations that she sexually abused her brother or struck him in any way." This is what Schaefer described in his confession. It seems to be in his memory, but is it really HIS memory? Or is it the childhood memory of a discarnate attached to him?

In every case of discarnate attachment or possession there are different individuals or groups with their own history, their own agenda, and often in great variety. Through conversation with them you can sort out who is who and which ones are the most dominant. Many are willing to converse—some require encouragement or special attention. ANY patterns of the host are automatically compromised or enhanced, by attachment.

Some of the hosts know of their passengers and some work with them, like a team. Others know and feel powerless to free themselves. All the other factors outside the self, such as those listed by Norris, have weakened the embodied human for easy possession by a very negative and controlling discarnate.

"Prevention & Cure Is Possible" Theory

Yes, prevention is possible. It would require effective intervention during childhood, to stop the destructive environmental situations with parents or caretakers, and an inquiry and/or clearing process if needed. The condition of the family environment in American society and the lack of acceptance of the concept of other-dimensional beings and how they affect our lives make this very difficult to achieve.

We, as practitioners, work with young people who are from abusive/dysfunctional homes. We educate them about multidimensional realities and how they can affect the body, mind and spirit. We teach them processes and how to use the "tools" as prevention or relief for any situation.

Connecting to one's inner being (three aspects of self) is the first step. It is a connecting to one's own spirit and divine nature. In this process of connection, we become linked to our higher guidance within self. This higher guidance provides a more expanded view of ourselves, and our environment, than does the self (kaho aka) that walks through our daily lives.

Clues and Detection

Norris states, "These serial murders are the ones in which the killer is compelled by forces beyond his control, and unless those forces are understood, the killer eludes detection."

The obvious clues are to be found in the list of symptoms I described earlier. Norris writes of the research of Vernon Mark of Harvard where he studies epileptic conditions in some serial killers. I feel that some of these conditions are the same as in conditions observed in cases of spirit attachment. There can be disruption in the electromagnetic field of the host when a discarnate is agitated or when there is some kind of incompatibility between the host and the discarnate. This disruption can manifest as an observable epileptic condition.

In any case, the symptoms of certain types of epilepsy (psychomotor or limbic) are identical to that of severe possession. The most profound example can be found with severe mental disorders. In regard to the lesions in or near the limbic cortex and other damage found in the brains of those with epilepsy, feelings of terror, fear, strangeness and unreality, sadness, paranoia and the need for isolation (as listed by Norris). I wonder which came first, the chicken or the egg—injury and subsequent attachment—or, attachment causing subsequent injury? More food for research.

Detection is very possible if limited thought is replaced by open minds on the part of the investigators. It can be accomplished by a psychic who is familiar with that process—or by a counselor or hypnotist, who is familiar with conversing with discarnates. In the book, *The Unquiet Dead*, by Dr. Edith Fiore, Dr. Fiore describes many of the encounters she has had as she utilizes hypnosis to communicate with entities that are attached to her clients. Although Dr Fiore has stated that she does not deal with demonic possession or spiritual issues, the goal of these sessions is to encourage the discarnates to release.

For obvious reasons, the anonymity of any "sensitive" working in the field of criminology is vital! The danger of retaliation is why more of us are not participating in this field, as well as the aversion most people have to the gruesome circumstances surrounding these cases.

In dealing with violent entities, I encourage working in a group session utilizing the methods I describe in earlier chapters. The process used for these types of situations is very important, as are the attitudes of those in attendance. Some of the work, or all of it, may be done without the host present, although each case must be evaluated independently before making that choice.

Awareness of the "Other"

The following information came from interviews with serial killers as written by Norris. "Lucas reveals that he had a long period of hallucinations during which he lost touch with reality while he was in prison in Michigan. He heard his dead mother's voice telling him to commit suicide and to commit murder, and when he asked for help from the prison medical authorities his request was turned down."

"...He explains that his killing episodes were always preceded by periods of heavy drinking after which he became almost stuporous. It was in this semi-stupor that he committed the vast majority of his homicides...When asked how he perceived his victim at the time of the murder, he explained: 'Its more of a shadow than anything else. You know it's a human being, but yet you can't accept it. The killin' itself, it's like say, you're walkin' down the road. Half of me will go this way and the other half goes that way. The right hand side didn't know what the left hand side was going to do.'"

I suggest in this case that the discarnate had easy access to full control over Lucas' behavior, as all inhibitions were dissolved by alcohol, leaving him a puppet for his homicidal resident(s).

In another case, Bobby Joe Long had not been violent prior to a motorcycle accident, where he received severe head injuries. He began to have sexual fantasies and he reported them to army doctors. They dismissed it. He became a rapist, prompted by these severe sexual fantasies.

There could have been an "inquiry" at that point, to see if he had taken on any discarnates from the accident/hospitalization, and a subsequent "release." Head injury can be the cause for altered behavior, but not always the only or even the main cause. Those with head injuries are almost always hospitalized, even for a brief time—and hospitals are a major location for attachment.

Norris writes, "Long explains that he never consciously wanted to hurt his victims but that he felt compelled to commit the rapes by a force inside him. He never understood it but was greatly afraid that the crimes would escalate unless he was able to muster the power to control his sexual urges."

Later, when the crimes did escalate, Long, like some others, left enough clues for the police to find him, and when he was captured he quickly began his confession. "He explained that he knew exactly what he was but that he had no control over the feelings that came upon him."

Norris tells of another killer, Carlton Gary. "Carlton Gary experienced the phases of a serial murderer through phantom figures that he generated in his own mind." In early years, prior to his crimes or prison, Gary also complained to medical authorities that he had "visions" of violent sex—his pleas were ignored. "Gary's confessions revealed that he was at the scene of every crime. However, he claims that he witnessed the crimes as they were committed, by another person. He watched from another room or from the street, but he was never there!!!"

These men were asking for help that wasn't there, but it can be. Please, what will it take? MAY I SUGGEST, each one was watching his own attached entities commit the crimes! People are able to move in and out of their bodies, this is common knowledge—they can also BE moved in and out of their own bodies by another! Whether the hosts moved away from repulsion, or were moved to prevent interference, it doesn't matter. It happened. It doesn't matter whether medical personnel can explain it or not—it happened. Belief in any of this is not required, it is happening anyway!

Many people leave their body intentionally, for various reasons. Meditation, curiosity, astral travel or pain relief. My sister uses self-hypnosis to go to a corner of the ceiling in her dentist's office to have her teeth filled. As a hypnosis regression therapist, I take clients out of their bodies to relieve stress or to view a traumatic situation floating above it, emotionally removed.

Just as we find with common possession, some hosts are aware of their attachments, even names and descriptions—others are not. In the case of Charles Manson, Norris writes, "He joined a number of religious and satanic cults to heighten the other-worldly sensations he was experiencing" Need I "suggest" anything???

So, Who Is Responsible?

I do not mean to imply that criminals dealing with spirits who manipulate their behavior are innocent just because someone else did it. In fact, we are each responsible for what happens to us or through us, whether it is unfinished business of past lives or present-life situations. I do believe we are responsible to expand and grow in our awareness, of the true reality of our lives, and make the necessary improvements to enhance the quality of our existence, or not.

Most criminals were victims first. We have to start somewhere and everywhere, to begin to assist a major healing process for all who are on the wheel of misery, which begets misery, abuse which begets more of the same and on and on. We must break the negative cycles and circles of suffering. Hopefully, there are some medical professionals willing to bridge the gap between science and spirit, because that is what it will take. In this country, we don't need more laws or prisons—we need more healing.

The overall picture of human behavior and spirit attachment is very extensive, complex and in some cases, even bizarre. But to ignore the reality of it is inexcusable and dangerous. Only when the whole picture is accepted, can we begin to plan preventative and correctional measures that can be implemented in family training and counseling programs and other human services already existing.

Family is the base for all other aspects of our lives. The family unit is the matrix for the human community and all other life. In this country, the "family" structure is in shambles for millions of people. This is not simply about divorced parents, it is about dysfunctional individuals, full of pain, anger and fear. Dysfunctional homes create dysfunctional people, people who become the community, the state, the country.

The most alarming aspect of American culture (or the lack of it) is the billions of dollars being made on the dysfunctional, unhealthy aspects of our society. Who is going to give up that income? The economic structure is a major cause for the deterioration of family life. Parents are often too drained from trying to provide the basic material needs to be able to give healthy attention and affection to their children.

The moral fibers are shredded—more fathers are seeding families they don't want to care for, leaving the burden on the mother. Mothers are having children they can't afford or don't want. Many Grandparents are less and less a part of the household, to assist in the care of the children, sharing their wisdom and maturity. Other Grandparents are burdened with rearing another whole generation of children, when they could be in their new adventures, rest and retirement years.

At the top of the list is a serious disconnection from "spirit," the spiritual aspect of our being, not religion, but spirit in the true sense of the word. A healthy connection to spirit teaches us about our own Divinity, our personal godliness. Within our very nature, when not in distortion, is the desire to love and be loved.

As society has become more focused on the material things of living, it has pulled away from spirit. People are comparing their "things" or "position", to other people's things or position. Consequently, many base their self-worth on their social/material worth. I suppose it is a natural human trait, which can be traced back to how good a hunter/provider a man was as a prospective mate/father.

Within a healthy tribal situation, the man would still have to be of good manners and integrity to be honorable—or the whole tribe or village would chastise him or run him out. He would be a disharmonious spirit causing displeasure from the gods and ancestors, which could cause crisis with weather, crops or other plights of nature. This would bring great stress upon the entire tribe or village—just as it is doing on a very large scale in this country. The tribal women would enjoy their roles and take pride in their skills, their homes and nurture their children

For a healthy, happy life, there can be no separation of body, mind and spirit of the individual. This extends into the family or group body/mind/spirit, which extends into the community body/mind/spirit. We are each a part of the whole, we are all connected in spirit. When one is in pain, we all feel it at one level or another.

You will find that love, in the true sense of the word, is what is missing in the serial killers of this world and the discarnates that may be attached to them. No one ever taught them about love.

Who Can Help?

Many of the symptoms in serial killers, both biological and behavioral may be explainable in medical terms by doctors and researchers, but I ask that you at least consider that many of these same symptoms are common in possession as well. In cases of MPDs there are even separate distinct brain patterns of the different "personalities." I suggest that it is in fact because they are different "people."

In the chapter, The New Criminologists (*Serial Killers*), Norris writes, "Scientists and doctors must understand that they are themselves impaired by a "linkage blindness," an inability to relate causalities in disparate professional disciplines to one another. Consequently, sociologists look for social causalities and find them; psychologists look for psychological and developmental causalities and find them; and neurologists look for organic causalities and identify them as well. The police and prosecutors simply brand criminals as "bad," track them down, and bring the few they find before the courts. However, each of the different professions is merely groping like a blindfolded person around the body of an elephant. Nobody can see the elephant and nobody recognizes that anybody else is there."

I agree with Norris that these linkages must be united to have the full picture of the "elephant," before a clear understanding of serial killers can be established. I ask that one more concept be added to the rest of what could be a team, with eyes and minds open and egos tucked away, and that is the concept of possession, a very present and often dangerous reality.

There is nothing magical or mystical about possession, it is a fact of life and death. It must not be explained away by medical, psychological, scientific or ecumenical conjecture. We practitioners of integrity must not be dismissed as kooks. I look forward to the day when medical professionals will show the effects of spirit possession, in their terms, on their charts. It already can be done. Any volunteers?

I wish to thank Joel Norris for his excellent study of serial killers and the book he wrote about them.

Many medical people will say I am wrong or nuts or both—that is fine—but what if I'm not? I am willing to participate in researching that question.

I close this chapter with a quote from Nikola Tesla:

"When science begins the study of non-physical phenomena, it will make more progress in one decade than in all the centuries of existence."

Huna—A Way of Life

In the Hawaiian language, subtle changes in pronunciation change the meaning of the words. Huna is a Hawaiian word pronounced hoo-nah, which means: to hide, conceal, disguise, secrete, confidential, covert. It refers to the "higher teachings" of the priests (Kahunas) of ancient Hawaii. My interpretation is that it was, and is, the practice of understanding and utilizing Universal Principles (see that chapter) to facilitate harmonious existence between all life forms and the natural elements that support life.

The esoteric code for these Natural Laws is actually hidden within the ancient words of the Hawaiian language, Hebrew and many other original tongues. They are no longer the same languages that you would find in modern dictionaries. The ancient Hawaiian language was never recorded, rather it was held in the minds of all who used it. Most of these people are gone, but some of the original meanings filtered down through chants, songs or those few elders (Kupunas) who still teach the ancient ways.

Why was the Huna code held and kept secret by the priests? Originally, it was to retain the clarity and purity of the information by keeping it from those who were not prepared to use it. Later, the teachings were suppressed for the same reason these same Light teachings (evident in many ancient cultures), were and still are being hidden from the masses—to keep the power of these teachings confined to the church or priestly elite, so they can retain control over their followers.

Huna is not to be considered a religion, but a way of life. In ancient times there was no separation between physical and spiritual existence. The reverence for the God aspect in all things was observed in the daily activities of life. What a great idea—peace and harmony seven days a week! One of the basic principles of Huna is that the psychological and spiritual aspects of the self are vital to the health of the whole person.

You will find that this information can be incorporated into many religions, philosophies or cultures and used by people of all ages. Children respond especially well to Huna teachings because they are not usually emotionally inhibited, or limited by negative thought patterns as many adults are.

I believe the origin of Huna as an original Light teaching began long before the existence of what we refer to as the Hawaiian culture. The essence of this psycho/spiritual philosophy can be found in many cultures and their spiritual teachings, including the Christian bible. I have found Huna to be the most simple, practical, clear and powerful way to translate the Universal Principles. It has been unfailing when utilized in all aspects of my personal and professional life.

The basic concept within the Huna philosophy is that all things have three aspects, a trinity in all things. All practices within the Huna system utilize this concept. The Hawaiian terms for these three aspects in humans are: Kino Aka, key-no ah-kah, Kaho Aka, kah-ho ah-kah and Makua Keahu, mah-koo-ah kay-ah-hoo. Modern clinical terms for these aspects are: Sub-conscious, Conscious, and Super-conscious, generally speaking.

In pre-missionary times, the ancient Hawaiians were referred to as the Mana Huna. The word Mana means supernatural or divine power, miraculous power, spiritual authority, privilege. That name and it's meaning were changed by others over time, to Menehune—a legendary race of little people.

Isn't it interesting that the languages of the Hawaiians, the Hopi, and the Nepalese are so similar? The feathered helmet headdress of the ancient Hawaiian is nearly identical to those worn in Nepal. It is also difficult to tell the differences in the visage of these peoples as well.

The ancient Hawaiians believed themselves to be the Original People on the planet. The Hawaiian Chant of Creation (Kumulipo) tells of their origin—the stars! The chant also tells of the time when the ancient Hawaiians lived on the land of Mu with the dinosaurs!

In ancient times, a Hawaiian person would go to a Kahuna for assistance with their various problems. Each Kahuna had a specific skill and some were multi-skilled. As incoming cultures influenced the Hawaiian culture, many of these practices were greatly altered or terminated completely. The first invasion was not of the White man, as many believe. It was by the Tahitian and Samoan people. At first there was mutual harmony. With the entry of Polynesian leaders who wanted power and control, the peaceful way of life faded. Most of what followed is written history.

I believe the Light Teachings are encoded within all of us. We just need to let in enough Light to dispel the shadows of false truths, which hide their message. Our earthly lives are for the purpose of remembering the ultimate message of all Light teachings—that Love is All—while mastering the limitations of physical existence. The Huna philosophy teaches that all things animate or inanimate have vibration (movement), and all are interrelated. There is only one basic rule to follow in Huna, never intend to cause harm to any person, place or thing—including the self!

How easy this would be…but in order to live this way, everyone would have to function from a clear heart. So now, we come to the tools that can clear the heart and bring balance and harmony to the body, mind and spirit. These tools can enable us to discover that ultimately, all that we need is within ourselves. One of the greatest teachers of this reality was Emmanuel (Jesus the Christed).

The tools that follow are in keeping with the basic Universal Principles in simple usable form. Some are known to be practices from ancient Hawaiian times, others are more modern, some of them are my inspired interpretation. They can be used a little or a lot. The more they are used, the greater the benefit. The tools can be used in all situations and can be simplified or elaborated upon.

In a perfect world there is no blame. We do not yet realize our perfection. So, where there is blame, there is a need for forgiveness, in order to heal and evolve. The main objective is FREEDOM and SELF-EMPOWERMENT and the RESPONSIBILITY that comes with it.

The key to the tools is Communication.

COMMUNICATION is the key to Understanding the self and others.

UNDERSTANDING is the key to Forgiveness and Love for the self and others.

LOVE is the HEALING.

The Three Aspects Of The Self

The concept of three predominant aspects of the self is accepted by modern psychology or psychiatry, however, there are many variations of opinion about the mechanics of the functions of the three selves within the person. An important point that most contemporary medical practitioners do not take into consideration is the existence of the multi-dimensional aspect of our selves. This closed place in their thinking limits them in their ability to facilitate complete healing.

Here is a list of terms that have been applied to the three selves by those who have written on the subject:

Sub-conscious	Conscious	Super-conscious
Id	Ego	Super Ego
Lower Self	Middle Self	Higher Self
Child	Mother	Father

Animal aspect...............	Mind aspect.................	God aspect
Computer......................	Programmer..................	Supervisor
Unihipili........................	Uhane...........................	Aumakua
Ku...............................	Lono............................	Aumakua

The terms I choose to use I will list here. I feel they are the most accurate of all from my research and been confirmed by several Hawaiian elders.

| kino aka........................ | kaho aka....................... | makua keahu |

I feel that the concept of the Christian Trinity (father, son and holy spirit/ghost) is derived from the ancient concept of the three selves. It was changed to the male-dominant terminology that removes one's Divinity from within the self, eliminates female Divinity completely, and places God outside of one's reach. Only through the assistance and approval of the clergy, could one have audience with God. This was done to remove power from the individual and place it in the hands of the priestly caste.

Many ceremonial prayers end with "In the name of the Father, the Son and the Holy Spirit/Ghost." Could this be a contaminated version of the original intention of always honoring and communicating with the three selves in order to demonstrate harmony and personal connection between the self and Divine Creator? I think so.

As you will see, the following processes address and honor the trinity of the self whether you are male or female. The Hawaiian terms of kino aka, kaho aka and makua keahu collectively, represent the Inner Family or three selves.

Here is an outline of the nature and functions of the three selves, as I have experienced them withinin myself and others. I suggest you begin to gather information from your own three selves on a regular basis. Each person is unique, so too are the other selves within. It can be a wonderful adventure and a very healing experience.

The Kino Aka

The kino aka can be thought of as the "child-like" nature of the self. It has been referred to as the sub-conscious, nature spirit, the obedient servant, or the idiot that will do anything you tell it to. One important function of the kino aka is to retain memory of all experience of all lifetimes and does this quite literally. It is deductively logical simply folowing "orders" without discernment. An example of this could be the following scenario: a seven-year old boy is excitedly running through the house, looking for dad, to show him the amazing lizard he found in the yard. The poor little guy slips and falls into a small table with a lamp on it. The lamp breaks, the boy feels a painful impact on his elbow and drops the lizard. The dad runs to the scene, yelling at the boy for being so stupid, destructive and, "you will be punished for breaking the rules, you know there is no running allowed in the house…!"

The boy is absorbing the words and the attitude of the dad very personally, as children do, but he is also in great pain and is very worried about possible injury and the whereabouts of the poor little lizard. It is obvious that dad is not concerned about the boy's injury or the welfare of the lizard. This too is painful to the boy. Which messages will be absorbed by the kino aka? What will be the memory of this event, shoved into the sub-conscious, until it happens again and again? Will it be the wonderful discovery of the amazing lizard? What will become a strong program in the subconscious, as the boy relates to himself as a person?? Hopefully, the child will grow up, get therapy and go on to be a wonderful veterinarian or herpitologist.

The kino aka is the instinctual self, which controls the automatic functions of the body. The kino aka never sleeps—it records continually. Another very important aspect of the kino aka is that it is the access to the higher self—the only access, end of subject! The relationship between the kaho aka and the kino aka is a direct reflection of the spiritual nature of person.

Some people believe the inner child could be separated from the body, or could leave. Others feel this is incorrect. The kino aka can seem to be separate or against you, but this is only when that aspect of a person is confused, neglected or abused. It does not actually disconnect from the body, but its essence can travel, as our ethereal bodies can travel, always connected by an ethereal cord.

The very first step in healing the emotional body is through the kino aka. The only access to "Spirit" is through the kino aka. This is step one, level one, for anyone who wishes to enlighten or expand their awareness.

Hypnosis and/or focused meditation are ways to contact the kino aka directly when communication to the kaho aka (conscious self) is closed, which can happen when the kaho aka blocks the inner feelings and information. Conscious communication with the kino aka comes easily when acknowledgement and trust are established through thoughtful interaction.

When we block inner guidance or warnings our physical body is affected. The blockages begin to settle in various organs and systems of the body and disease is created. The connection to our makua keahu (higher self) is strangled and our divine higher guidance and energy to heal is shut down. We become self destructive at a sub-conscious level, one part at a time. Some choose to cover their inner feelings and information with alcohol or drugs, which can accelerate the destruction process.

Chronic negative thoughts and feelings which cause emotional dysfunction and disease are anger, guilt, bitterness, jealousy, sorrow, grief, worry, contempt and judgement, to name a few. The emotion that is underlying all contrary feelings is excessive and/or distorted fear. The kino aka can show you the source of the blockages so they can be transformed. Here is held the memories of everything that has ever happened to you in this, or past lives. Most of the traumas are from past programming or experience. A blockage is created when a trauma is not resolved within and released—when fear, pain and anger are stuffed and ignored. Even small hurts accumulate into larger ones when they are repeated over and over.

The kino aka can also be a warning system through innate, instinctive wisdom. The memories held here and the access to the higher self enable the kino aka to have a better picture of your patterns than the kaho aka (conscious self). Learn to communicate between your three selves in the same way a ship requires teamwork between Captain and crew to sail smoothly.

The Kaho Aka

The kaho aka can be thought of as the parent-like aspect or the Captain of the ship. It has the spirit/will to direct, to focus it's attention on something. It has navigational control of the physical body. There is also the ability to make choices or decisions with discernment and the ability to ignore or suppress the mental and/or emotional reaction to what it sees, hears or feels. I call it the one who thinks it knows everything, but is often full of other people's information, which may or may not be good.

The kaho aka has been referred to as the Conscious self and has reasoning ability, intuition, emotional feeling and creative thought. It gives the orders, is vocal and has the ability to learn, expand consciousness and experience the physical senses. How the kaho aka MANIFESTS all of these abilities is in "direct" relationship to the inner translation received and recorded by the kino aka. We can see the condition of that relationship in the outer persona of an individual. Let's look at how it works.

A beautiful young woman is quite pre-occupied with her physical appearance and not concerned about much else. Her desire is to "marry the perfect man, have two children and live in comfort and security, happily ever after." This is what was strongly impressed upon her as a child growing up. She was also told very often and by many that she was so pretty. She was harassed by her mother to stay that way by focusing on her diet, cosmetics, wardrobe and all that staying "pretty" entails—that it was the most important thing about becoming a "desir-able" woman. This is how she would find her perfect husband who would take good care of her and her two children.

There was little emphasis placed on any other aspect of being a desirable "per-son." Consequently, this young woman has had a long string of affairs with men and is in great confusion about the emptiness within herself. Her second marriage is in shambles and her female friends consider her a threat. Hopefully she will get therapy to undo the superficial program that is running at her sub-conscious (kino aka) level. Perhaps she can become the real person that is buried under her mother's influence on the kaho aka.

The Makua Keahu

The makua keahu can be thought of as the higher guardian/parent self or per-sonal source of inspiration from within: more simply, the god self. It communi-cates on all levels, via dreams, telepathic thoughts, visions, through other people, animals or objects. The higher self can communicate directly through meditation or other altered states of consciousness. This aspect knows us better than any other self and has the overview our entire life blueprint. The makua keahu sus-tains our body, mind and spirit for our lifetime. It does this from the level of Universal Principles and the life plan that you, as an unborn soul/spirit, created before incarnating into present body.

The makua keahu does not give orders—it does give guidance. It has the abil-ities of the kino aka, the kaho aka and more. From this level we have the ability to access the heavenly realms for higher wisdom. The makua keahu sees into our future and into our past. It is our soul/mind aspect. It has direct connection to all of our Spirit Guides—it is our personal Divine Guidance. The essence of this aspect is within and without, extending and expanding, merging with the greater "All that is."

Some believe our god-self exists outside, above the physical body. I feel this viewpoint is due to old programming that godliness and human-ness are sepa-rate…that one is inferior to the other…that god is up there and we are down

here. I believe God is everywhere, all-pervasive, all-encompassi.
that one is aware of their own god-aspect depends upon their pei
ship with the two other "selves."

The makua keahu is unlimited and impersonal. Some refer tc   _akua
keahu as our Angelic guardian self, others refer to it as our Star self. Any specific
description of another persons' makua keahu is speculation. One can only discover this knowledge by communicating with and between the selves.

BEING DIS-CONNECTED FROM THE THREE SELVES CAN MANI-
FEST THIS WAY...

The kino aka takes in information but is withdrawn and in confusion.
The kaho aka thinks it has all the information (but doesn't).
The makua keahu can't get any messages of assistance through.

BEING CONNECTED WITH THE THREE SELVES CAN MANIFEST
THIS WAY...

The kino aka takes in information and gives it back upon request.
The kaho aka gathers information, consults the kino aka for feedback
and remains open to guidance from the makua keahu.
The makua keahu is always able to assist through the clear channel.
The kaho aka gives acknowledgement and gratitude to all three selves.
Harmony, health and balance are created—Joy is the result.
Now, let us take our power back and form our own personal connection to
our three selves to better understand and communicate with our own true nature.
The way to begin is with our relationship to our inner child (kino aka), who is
the "key" to actualizing the divine nature of our inner and outer world. The inner
child is the only direct link to our divine god-self....and a child shall lead them.

The Toolbox

Using The Tools

COMMUNICATION is the key—LANGUAGE is the means—THE POWER is in the INTENT. The intent must be clear and focused. Intent is the desire, the want/will. Get excited about your process—make a big deal of it. The kino aka is strongly impressed by drama and animation. Did you ever notice how children are mesmerized by television commercials? These are always a dramatization of a message. Manufacturers are very aware of the emotional and psychological effect of their advertising. They constantly utilize the most powerful techniques to grab the consumer.

Your desire is measured by how much you want something, coupled with your belief that the desired thing is attainable. This is in direct relationship to whether you feel you are worthy or deserve it. This you can discover by observing and communicating with your kino aka, as it mirrors your inner self. It will show you what and where any blockages may be. As children, we were very impressionable, especially regarding our parents or other authority figures. Some of those impressions may not be healthy, and can be altered. So much of our information comes from other people's viewpoints. When programs are repeatedly being recorded by the kino aka, they become crystallized patterns of behavior.

As adults we may find we need to change the patterns that do not serve our highest good. I say change because the universe is not a vacuum—nothing is eliminated—it only changes form. NOTHING is eliminated. There is only transformation and transmutation...and we are our own universe within a universe. We can change the patterns...from dark to light, from sad to happy, from sick to well, from hate to love, from poverty to prosperity, from limitation to freedom.

And now, to begin with the first two tools. These are also your greatest tools and will assist you in using all others. They are: The Creative Imagination and A Sense of Humor. If you are a little rusty on either of these, practice! To create is to express—to laugh is to heal.

This first section of the Toolbox contains what I consider to be the basic tools for anyone who wishes to explore all aspects of the self as related in the concepts presented in this book. When a client asks me, "Where do I begin?" I refer them to these first steps.

Preparation For All Journeys And Processes

The state you are in is very important in doing any introspection, prayer or other ceremony with the self or with others. These types of procedures are for communing with the Divine Soul/Spirit nature of our selves or others. Reverence is the attitude to embrace, not fearful tension, rather, light, joyful, playful reverence. Be responsible, because you are. Treat the self and others as sacred beings. Treat the time you spend in any of these procedures as a sacred circle of energy. Call upon your personal Divine Guidance to assist you.

The term I use (personal Divine Guidance) refers to ALL ethereal beings who comprise our Divine team of guides, collectively. They include our higher-self, our guardian ancestors, our Angelic assistants and any other-dimensional beings who are part of each person's team of "Spirit Guides" (the most common term). For me, this refers only to beings who are in harmony with Divine Christ or Buddhic vibration. They too, encourage joy and play. Ask them to assist you in creating that "sacred space" for yourself. Once a process is complete always thank them for their assistance.

Be physically comfortable without putting yourself to sleep. Be free of any drugs or alcohol that distort your personal truth. Secure your area from any interruption (doorbell, telephone, etc.). Wear loose comfortable clothing. Prepare yourself and your space for your ceremonies, your personal medicine. Afterwards, you may need to drink some water and rest before resuming your daily activities.

These tools can be recorded onto an audio or video tape to use as your narration. You can do these processes alone or with someone. Two people can take turns or one can narrate to a group. Participants must not be critical in any way during these sessions. Caring and supportive understanding is the required atmosphere.

Visualization is not important. We all receive information through various senses. Those who have difficulty visualizing at first will eventually be able to, with practice and relaxation of mind. Let us practice a little now: What was the last bright red object you saw? What color is the top cover on your bed? What color are your bathroom walls, the floor, your kitchen walls? What color is your favorite shirt? What does it look like? Some people visualize with their eyes open while focusing on any one object, like daydreaming. What kind of car would you really like to have or have already? Really see it!

Often, the thing we visualize comes in quickly and fades quickly. That is fine. The image is stored in your memory to recall. Don't expect an 8 X 10 glossy.

Allow the experience to flow, don't analyze any of it until it is complete! Be open to new awareness and trust.

Basic Tools

The Breath of Ha (the breath of life)

I suggest that the "Breath of Ha" be the first part of any ceremony, prayer or process done in healing or communication with Spirit. It is a preparation of the body, mind and spirit to relax, unite and focus. This is a modified version and can be extended to seven times or more for deep meditation. Breathe and count at your own pace, whatever is comfortable for you.

(NARRATE):
Inhale (COUNTING TO 7 MENTALLY)
Hold   "   "
Exhale "   "
Hold   "   "
Relax and breathe normally.
(REPEAT 3 MORE TIMES)
Relax, clearing the mind and body of all tension, relax, relax…

Practice this until you have memorized the procedure and developed a comfortable timing for your counting.

An Introduction To Your Kino Aka

This process was given through me, by a Hawaiian spirit guide who is always with me. I have used it with individuals and groups, personally and professionally, with great success. It can be a very powerful experience. Read through the entire journey first. Decide if you feel comfortable using it yourself or with a friend(s) or you can consult an appropriate practitioner to assist you.

Items Of Importance

It does not matter what form the inner child takes, initially. Some have come forward as animals, adults, E.T.'s or even objects. These manifestations can be symbolic or actual entities. The ultimate true form of the inner child is one's self as a child or teen. Sometimes, the child will not look like you at all, or even be of your same gender or race, or there may be more than one child. A process of elimination is done in these situations. To obtain the truth, ask this question with a firm statement: ARE YOU, IN FACT, MY (NAME, IF OTHER PERSON) KINO AKA? If there is a long hesitation or the answer is anything other than yes, then they are NOT.

A child that does not look like you is either yourself (male or female) in a past lifetime and will answer yes, or a discarnate child (or children) that is attached to you. When it is a discarnate, gentle, friendly communication will disclose this. You can ask them if they know they are deceased—if not, encourage them to look into their memory and see what happened. Comfort them accordingly and call upon Archangel Michael to safely release them into Divine Light. Read the chapters on Exorcism or the Toolbox to assist you.

If the being is an animal, it could be a pet or a totem animal of your own. If it is neither one of these, it is probably an intruder. Call upon Archangel Michael to provide protection while you converse with it, or to come and release it from you. Use whatever tools you feel are appropriate. If it is a deceased pet, ask if it is ready for release and encourage this process. If it is a totem animal, ask what message it has for you and give thanks.

If the being looks like an E.T. or other non-earthly type of being, it very well could be. Use the same procedure of asking it what it wants. If you do not feel comfortable about the entity, call upon Archangel Michael for protection and to place the entity into containment. At that point, you can use the Ho'oponopono Process and ask for a release to be completed. If you feel the need to know more about the being's identity or purpose, I suggest you solicit a practitioner who is adept at this kind of communication and release. Benevolent E.T.'s do not intrude into this process.

Finally, if an object is presented through the center of the flower, rather than your child, it is usually symbolic. Ask if it is a symbolic message from your child. Some are very shy, at first, and don't want to show themselves. Ask them to just show you one hand through the flower. Then, ask them to wiggle their fingers. If they respond to this, you have made contact and I encourage gentle communication, briefly each day until the child feels safe and there is a comfortable rapport.

Think of a resistant child as a traumatized child and begin to ascertain the nature of the trauma. Simple language in small doses, there is no rush, until you are both comfortable companions. That is the ultimate goal.

(NOTE TO NARRATOR) Read this material first to familiarize yourself with the process. Directions for you are in parenthesis and capitalized. Say the words with feeling. Practice reciting the journey beforehand.

The Rainbow Journey

(NARRATE): The kino aka may be male or female, human or other type of being or inanimate object, so don't have any expectations. Some of you may have already seen your child but perhaps you didn't know who it was. The term "child" is used only because it represents the "child-like" aspect of us, but it may not appear in that form. Treat this experience like a reunion, with gentleness and understanding.

(NARRATE AT MODERATE SPEED, USE A CALM SOOTHING TONE, PAUSING BETWEEN EACH STEP—YOU CAN COUNT ALOUD IF IT ASSISTS THE GROUP SYNCHRONICITY, OR EACH PERSON CAN COUNT ON THEIR OWN, MENTALLY.)

"Let us begin with the Breath of Ha" (complete that process)

Now we begin our journey.

All the colors of the rainbow are in the atmosphere, in the ethers and we can access them any time we wish. Now, let us open our inner vision and see that every color in the rainbow is now floating through your entire auric field—which extends beyond the physical body, from two to ten or more feet.

Now close your eyes and see the color red surrounding you, beautiful, rich, ruby red.

Now, inhale the color red and breathe normally and feel the red moving through your entire body…Feel the stimulating energy of the vibration of red, filling every cell, every atom in your entire body. Feel a stimulation at the base of your spine and feel that energy rooting into the earth beneath you, relax.

And now, as you exhale, see the red of your auric field turning into orange, beautiful, vibrant, sunset orange.

Now, inhale the color orange and breathe normally…feel the orange moving through your entire body…feel the warmth of the orange filling every cell, every atom in your entire body…feel a slight stimulation at the navel, enhancing your creative center, gently activating your seat of power.

And now, as you exhale, see the orange in your auric field turning into yellow, beautiful, bright, canary yellow.

Now, inhale the color yellow and breathe normally...feel the yellow moving through your entire body...feel the glow of sunlight filling every cell, every atom in your entire body...feel a slight stimulation in your solar plexus, you center stomach, the seat of your emotions and the source of your intuition, as it opens to balance feelings.

And now as you exhale, see the yellow in your auric field turning into green, beautiful emerald forest green.

Now, inhale the color green and breathe normally...feel the green moving through your entire body...feel the healing energy filling every cell, every atom of your entire body...feel a slight stimulation in your heart as it opens to give and receive love.

And now as you exhale, see the green in your auric field turning into blue, beautiful royal sapphire blue.

Now, inhale the color blue and breathe normally...feel the blue moving through your entire body...feel the cool, calming vibration of blue filling every cell, every atom of your entire body...feel a slight stimulation at the throat as it opens for self-expression.

And now as you exhale, see the blue in your auric field turning into purple, beautiful amethyst purple.

Now, inhale the color purple and breathe normally...feel the purple moving through your entire body...feel your spirit soaring as it is nourished by the rich spirit vibration of purple as it is filling every cell, every atom of your entire body...feel a slight stimulation of your third eye as it opens to your psychic vision.

On your next exhale, see the purple in your auric field turning into violet, beautiful vibrant violet.

Now, inhale the violet and breathe normally...feel the violet moving through your entire body...feel the transformational vibration of a cool violet flame moving up through the center of your inner being to the crown of your head, as it gently opens your crown to access Divine Creator.

On your next exhale, see the violet in your auric field turning into pink, beautiful soft rose pink.

Now, inhale the pink and breathe normally...feel the pink moving through your entire body...feel the soft, warm love vibration of rose pink filling your heart. Fill your body with that rose pink love energy and see it wrapping completely around the outside of your body like a cozy, soft blanket. Remain in this vibration as we continue.

Now, just in front of you…see a beautiful white cloud, floating at eye level…a billowy white cloud.

Now, in the center of the cloud…see your very favorite flower—see the color and smell the aroma, if it has a fragrance.

We now speak to the kino aka(s). We are not here to criticize you, punish you or force you to do anything you do not wish to do. We do wish to meet you and communicate with you. I ask that you prepare to do this now.

Let us all concentrate on the center of the flower…as I now request of the kino aka(s) to peek your head through the center of the flower, so that we can see your face, the color of your hair, the color of your eyes. Now, I ask the kino aka(s) to put both hands through the center of the flower…and now, pull yourself through the center of the flower. Let us say hello, mentally or aloud…and see if there is a reply.

Now hug the child gently, if they allow it sharing love as you reunite. (PAUSE, TO GIVE TIME FOR INTERACTION, THEN CONTINUE NARRATION)

Now let us share with each other. If you do not wish to verbalize, you may remain quiet as we continue. We will begin with the first person to my left (or partner).

(ASK ONE QUESTION AND WAIT FOR AN ANSWER. RESPOND AS YOU SEE FIT, THEN CONTINUE. IF SOMEONE BECOMES UPSET DURING THE SESSION, ENCOURAGE THEM TO RELEASE THE EMOTION BY CRYING OR SHARING THEIR FEELINGS.)

Is your child male, female, or other?

How old is he/she?

What color hair does he/she have?

What color are his/her eyes?

What is he/she wearing, if anything?

Does he/she wish to say anything?

Now, I would like to ask your child, "What is your name? Would you share it with us? What do you wish to be called?"

Thank you, it is very nice to meet you.

I speak directly to you (the child) now to ask a simple but important question. Are you, in fact, _____ 's kino aka? Yes or No?

(IF IT IS NOT, FOLLOW PREVIOUS INSTRUCTIONS—IF YES, PROCEED)

We now call upon your Divine Guidance to present you with a beautiful Bubble Ship for protection and travel. See it now as a clear bubble floating in front of you. It is yours to keep, if you wish. You can make it any color you wish or change the color as you desire. You can change it to a solid, where no one can see into it. You can make it mirrored on the outside to reflect away any scary people or things.

This is your own private vehicle, you can travel anywhere you wish—you can bring someone with you. You can put anything inside that you need. You can make it as small or as large as you need, just as you can do with yourself.

Do you wish to keep it? (and if so) You can move into it now, simply by thought. You can navigate it by thought, as well. We now give thanks to Divine Guidance for this gift. (IF IT IS REFUSED, SAY, IT WILL BE THERE IF DESIRED).

(NEXT PERSON, CONTINUE UNTIL ALL HAVE BEEN ADDRESSED—END NARRATION.) At this point you can take a short break, then share the information in the following section. Please do not drive a car until you are re-adjusted to full consciousness.

More About Your Kino Aka

If you are disturbed by the child's appearance or behavior, it is temporary. The kino aka demonstrates what your inner self is feeling. This process can represent the first contact after many years or lifetimes. The condition of your child can show you the result of that lack of communication. The isolation is usually caused by emotional trauma that was not processed or released. Healing can begin at once, by giving love and concern to your kino aka.

Your kino aka most often appears as yourself in this lifetime, when you were a young child—the age varies. The age that your child manifests is usually the age you were at the time of an incident that caused trauma. Ask your child to take you to that time and identify it and put it into perspective for the present. Use any of the tools to assist in releasing the trauma. As this trauma is healed, the child will usually alter its age accordingly.

If your child is a different race than you and/or wearing clothing from another time—this is a sign that you lost touch with it in a past life and there has been a long separation. Proceed, as above, and go back to identify the situation. As the trauma heals, the child will usually alter its form to the present life. The point is to renew your relationship with your inner child and not let it deteriorate again. Basic common sense is all that is required in exploring your inner self. Keep it simple, one step at a time. There is no rush.

The more severe the isolation, the more patience and understanding may be required to heal the relationship. Always bathe in the pink love energy when working with a traumatized kino aka. You can request an Angelic companion for your child, to stay with them for as long as they wish. These are usually the same size as the child. Ask the makua keahu for assistance in the healing process. There is much to learn about our inner selves—your kino aka is the key to that understanding.

Remember the quote from the bible? Except ye "…become as little children, ye shall not enter into the kingdom of heaven." Matthew 18:3. I believe it means that only when we connect to our child-self, do we access our god-self.

Our kino aka is an aspect of our inter-dimensional nature and has freedom of movement within these realms. Don't be surprised if your child wishes to dress in a strange manner, or not at all—or wishes to take you traveling (mentally). Your child may also have strange requests, for example: wanting you to go someplace or do something you don't normally do. If so, do it with him/her, you could have a wonderful adventure. Your kino aka may also warn you about something, so listen to him/her—such as, "Don't go in that direction today." It could be a warning of an accident, delay, or bad timing. Our kino aka often reflects the intuitional aspect of our nature.

Ask him/her to show you their living quarters (so to speak). He/she may want to take you back with them, through the flower they emerged from during the "Journey." This can be very revealing as to your inner desires or inhibitions. We find that most kino akas enjoy rocking with us in a rocking chair, which they can manifest (in your mind), if you ask them to. You can also use yours, if you have one (physical). This can be very comforting when there is a need to balance and relax. If you are having trouble with the concept of an ethereal world, then you are probably having trouble relating to your child-self. Look beyond this physical world—that is where the rest of you is!

Your kino aka may seem to leave you for a while (this is not a disconnection) to go and visit elsewhere. Myself and others have had this experience. I did a speaking engagement in Honolulu for a day and a friend told me later that her kino aka told her she was going with me, and did. On another occasion I was in a very emotionally painful state, doing something I didn't want to do, and my child literally flew into a friend's house and said she wanted to stay there and play with her child—which she did for the rest of the afternoon.

When you need to communicate with someone but can't, for one reason or another, you can ask your kino aka to go and speak to that person's kino aka to give or receive information. All of the kino akas have their own telepathic link-up between each other. An example of this is: One day, the kino akas of our group wanted a beach party—a children's party. We all wanted to experiment. So, we agreed that all plans for the party would be done, only by the "children." We did not use telephones or verbal communication to choose the food and supplies. We had a wonderful party, with a balanced menu (pot luck). The main course was hot dogs, two types of salad, beverages and MANY desserts, of course. The kino akas also wanted to be baptized together in the ocean, and so they were!

When asking the kino aka for information, you can establish a preferred method such as, them showing you mental videos—many even have their own viewing room for you. Others use computers, inner voice, whole thought forms, or direct visual and audio (mentally). They have total access to all of our memory, from all lives, stored in our akashic records.

We can also communicate to the kino aka of another by asking permission and with the intention of higher service to that person. Choose a quiet place where you will not be disturbed. Calm your mind and create a nice mental environment to bring a guest. Then focus on the person you wish to contact. See their face in your mind and ask them if you can speak with their child. Then, ask your kino aka to go and fetch theirs. I did this with a friend whose kino aka started to bite me. I pulled him away quickly and asked my child to rock him in her chair to calm him. I gently counseled him but told him he did not have permission to abuse me as he had done to his (earthly) mother. This was a clear message for me to be aware of the anger and trauma of that individual which was carried form childhood. An abused child can bring those patterns into adulthood but that child can also be healed, by working with the kino aka.

What a great gift they (we) are—love them and thank them often. This is an excellent way to treat our physical children as well!

Connecting to Your Higher Self

Once you have established a comfortable balance with your inner child I suggest you complete the triangle of unity with your inner family by connecting to your higher self. The following process also came through me from my Hawaiian Spirit Guide. It is a journey where you, the conscious self (kaho aka), join your inner child (kino aka) in his or her Bubble Ship on the "Spiral Journey" to your higher self (makua keahu). Ask your kino aka ahead of time if he or she would take you on the Spiral Journey. It is through the "child" that we connect to our higher self. Ask the kino aka to prepare and let you know what would be the best time for both of you to take this journey together. Then prepare yourself for the rendezvous.

This process seems to denote that the god-self is "outside" of us. In reality, it is within and all around us, always. However, it is common thought that things of a godly/heavenly nature come from "above." I believe this journey to a star process is for ease of relating to and experiencing our godly nature.

(NOTE TO NARRATOR): Read this material first to familiarize yourself with the process. Directions for you are in parenthesis and capitalized. Say the words with feeling, practice reciting the journey beforehand. You can choose to use the English or Hawaiian words for each of the selves.

The Spiral Journey

(NARRATE AT MODERATE SPEED, USE A CALM SOOTHING TONE) We begin with the Breath of Ha. When that is completed begin to relax your entire body starting with the feet. Feel the relaxing power moving up through your entire body—FEEL your feet and legs relaxing, FEEL your thighs and hips relaxing—now FEEL the relaxing power moving up into your back muscles, moving up into your shoulders and down your arms and out your fingers—now FEEL your neck relaxing and FEEL your jaw muscles relax completely—now FEEL the relaxing power moving into your scalp and all around to your facial muscles—now FEEL your facial muscles relax completely. Your entire body is now completely relaxed.

We now ask your higher god-self (makua keahu) to activate the bright blue-white star shape of it's own energy floating high in space above your physical body.

We now call upon your inner child (kino aka). Greet the child and exchange any communications between you and move into the Bubble Ship. You and the ship will automatically become the appropriate size to accommodate both of you—I will be quiet for a while. (ALLOW A LITTLE TIME FOR THIS).

I speak to both of you now and ask you to take a deep breath and from your heart center, begin to fill yourselves and the Bubble Ship with beautiful, soft rose pink love Light. As you give each other a hug, the pink love Light expands to fill the Bubble Ship.

Look high above you and see the beautiful blue-white star. We ask your child (kino aka) to slowly move the Bubble Ship outside the physical body, then upward, spiralling in a clockwise direction around the outside of your body. As you move out and upward you will still be connected to your body by a thin elastic silver cord. It will mark your flight path. Continue this flight upward, and as you go beyond the body...focus on the star...it is waiting for you.

As you move in spiral flight toward the star, the sky becomes darker and darker until it looks like the black of the cosmos, with only that one blue-white star. As you move closer to the star, it becomes larger and larger, brighter and brighter. As you approach the source of your god-self (makua keahu) Light, take a deep breath...and when you are ready, move into the center of the star...(ALLOW SOME TIME FOR THIS).

FEEL the love/light energy of its beautiful blue-white Light...FEEL the joy that overwhelms you. You may want to release tears of emotion. Continue to breathe deeply as you and your child (kino aka) merge with this incredible godly aspect of yourselves...remain...bathing in the Light. Allow this powerful Love/Light essence of your being to magnify...expanding as far as it will. I will be quiet for a while (ALLOW SOME TIME FOR THIS).

Now, in your expanded state of radiance, you three are one. A Divine Soul/Spirit with an unlimited ability to create your own reality. You are in a Lighted state of full empowerment...acknowledge this truth about your self. Accept your own Divinity.

You are going to begin the journey back to the physical body now, together retaining all of your radiance. We ask the child (kino aka) to follow the same spiral pattern, which is marked by the silver cord, back to your body. Move at a moderate speed and as you approach your body, slow gently. When you reach the top of the head, see the crown chakra. It looks like a large lotus flower with many petals. See them opening to receive you. Gently lower the Bubble Ship through the crown into the body. The Bubble Ship will adjust in size.

The radiance of your Light will expand through and beyond your body as you settle at the center of your solar plexus (stomach). Now, FEEL that same energy permeate your entire body, healing and rejuvenating each and every cell, every atom. Allow this feeling to continue while I am quiet for a while (ALLOW TIME FOR THIS).

Finally, it is time to give thanks to your child (kino aka) and your god-self (makua keahu) for their participation in your journey. We ask each of you to now adjust your soul/spirit energy to return to your earthly functions. Allow your conscious self (kaho aka) time to come into balance with this adjustment. When you first begin to move your body, do it slowly and carefully. Please do not drive a car until you have adjusted to full consciousness.

(AT THIS POINT, ALL CAN TAKE A BREAK AND RESUME WITH DISCUSSION OR SHARING—END NARRATION).

Next Steps

At this point, I suggest you decide if you wish to complete the process between the inner selves, by going through the first Ho'oponopono process in the next chapter. Some of you may prefer to spend more time getting re-acquainted with your kino aka and makua keahu before you do this. Do what you are most comfortable with.

The following process can be a powerful catalyst in the clearing away of misunderstandings and imbalances between your three selves that currently exist or that may arise in the future.

Ho'oponopono—Between Your Three Selves

The Hawaiian word Ho'oponopono is pronounced ho-o-po-no-po-no. It means to rectify or correct an error or wrong that was done, to bring balance and harmony (pono) back to a situation or relationship. Being in "pono" is being in integrity with nature or Divine Law, being in balance and harmony. It is a process that was used by ancient Hawaiians to settle and release problems within relationships. The whole family or families of the involved persons were included in the process, as well as ancestors, spirit guardians and the Gods themselves. The reason for this all-encompassing practice was due to their belief that all things are related. A disturbance, between members of a family or families can throw a whole family or community out of balance. We refer to families, here because this was the main focus in Hawaiian lifestyle. The process can apply to any individuals or groups. The Ho'oponopono process was used to restore and maintain balance for the harmony of the whole, which is especially important in an island community anywhere.

This process is still used by many native Hawaiians and others. It can be a very powerful process and must be used with integrity. The word itself, Ho'oponopono, is very ancient and carries great power. There is a specific format that is still used today, however, the variations for a given situation are unlimited. In our spirit release work we use these tools to rectify and clear issues between our clients and those that are attached.

This process can also be used on objects, especially where any kind of mechanism is involved, such as, cars, boats, other vehicles or vessels, computers, etc. Often, these objects need to be energetically rebalanced because of human energies or entities that can affect them. A Hawaiian teacher told us of a large corporate computer she had cleared with this process. The computer was out of balance from the numerous human energies connected to the programmers and technicians. There was no other mechanical reason for the failure in its functioning.

Ho'oponopono, as a mediation process, is led by a practitioner or a respected elder in the family. It begins with a prayer (pule) or request for blessings and assistance from the Creator and Guardian Spirits (aumakua). This puts everyone into their heart, so to speak. Then, time is spent outlining the procedure that will be used. The next part of the process is to discuss the actual problem. This can resemble the peeling away of the layers of an onion, one at a time, until discovery of original cause comes to light. Strong aggressive emotions are diffused by the mediator, with care, to avoid arguing, as it solves nothing.

The participants are encouraged to be honest—judgement and blame are discouraged. If needed, there is a pause for relaxation of emotions called by the mediator. Then, a continuation until it is done. Some of the more complex situations can take days. Finally, an evaluation of the procedure is given and a new bonding is encouraged for all, through forgiveness. When it is finished, it is a thing of the past—not ever to be discussed again. A final prayer of gratitude and the sharing of food, finally bonds together all persons involved.

I have had the privilege of mediating in this process under varied circumstances. It is being used in the family court system and in business situations here in Hawaii. It is a most powerful tool. It can be used between the three inner selves or between the self and any other person, place or thing. I use it as my own personal daily process and teach it to others. As a crisis counselor, it is my predominant professional tool.

This process is used to begin to eliminate guilt, pain and fear—to bring our three selves into harmony. ALLOW yourself to FEEL this as you do it—our FEELINGS need to be healed first. The power of the Ho'oponopono is in the WORD and the INTENT of the individual. This can be a powerful catalyst, so be sure you are ready to take responsibility for your lives—all of them! You can decide this through introspection before you begin. Sections 2 through 5 can be recited by one, on behalf of all, or all can recite, one line at a time.

The Process

1. The Breath of Ha (complete that process)

2. (NARRATE FROM THIS POINT ON) "Divine Creator and all Divine Beings who assist me, I request your attention to witness and to bless this Ho'oponopono Process."

3. "Makua keahu (higher self) and kino aka (child self)—I now request of you, FORGIVENESS, for all errors of ALL our lives, past and present. I request that we three become united as ONE…IN DIVINE LOVE…and allow it to express through us in all areas of our existence both personal and universal. I request that all of our affairs be set into the Law of Right Action. I invoke the power within us to be of service to the Higher Good of our Selves and All others. I acknowledge our worthiness of abundance and prosperity. I humbly accept my own Divinity and the responsibility that it carries. I now invoke the transmutation of all disharmonious vibrations, to Pure Light. I request the release of any discarnate earthbound souls/spirits on or around me, into Pure Light, in the name of the Divine Christ energy…And it is done."

4. TO AFFIRM—(IF NARRATOR IS RECITING, HAVE ALL RECITE EACH LINE OF PRAYER AFTER YOU)

(Ancient Hawaiian prayer)

I AM THE I

"I come forth from the void into Light,

I am the breath that nurtures Life.

I am that emptiness, that hollowness beyond all consciousness,

The I, the Id, the All.

I draw my bow of rainbows across the waters,

The continuum, of minds with matters.

I am the incoming and outgoing of breath,

The invisible, untouchable breeze,

The indefinable atom of creation…I AM THE I."

5. I now acknowledge and give thanks to all who are present, of all time/space dimensions, of all vibrations. We are free…and it is done!

6. (TO CLEAR) At this time you bathe in water as a final cleansing. This can be done actually, in any body of water or symbolically, by sprinkling water or visualizing water flowing over you. Create this in any form that feels right to you.

After using this process for a number of weeks, I began to invoke the process daily by simply stating, "I now invoke the entire Ho'oponopono Process between myself and my inner family." I mentally ask if there are any matters to clear before completion. Then I make my statement of forgiveness and, "It Is Done." Afterwards, I speak to my kino aka about current events or ask my makua keahu for assistance, personal or professional, when it is needed. I always do this process, and the process between myself and my clients, prior to doing work with them.

When you have completed the Rainbow Journey and the Ho'oponopono Process between the three selves, you have established a good foundation for inner communication. This relationship can become stronger and more harmonious as you continue to use these procedures.

Ho'oponopono—Between Self and Others

As you create harmony within the self, you will become more aware of disharmonious situations and relationships around you—within your home, your circle of friends, or your working environment. The purpose of the next two processes is to clear and release all feelings that create disharmony between yourself and other persons (in body or out of body), places or things. I suggest you do any of these processes when you feel ready, in your own timing, whether you do one or more at a time.

ALWAYS DO THE HO'OPONPONO PROCESS BETWEEN YOUR THREE SELVES BEFORE DOING ANY PROCESS BETWEEN YOURSELF AND OTHERS. This assists you in being centered and balanced from within. This is a good place to be when encountering any "new" person, place or thing. We never know what karmic connection we may have had to any of these in the past.

Aka Cords

Negative feelings, conscious or unconscious, can involve undesirable connections to or from another person. The Hawaiian term for these psychic cords is "aka cords." These cords are actual strings of etheric substance hooked into one or more chakra points (energy centers) of the body. They can be as thin as spaghetti or the size of a small tree trunk! I have seen psychic paintings of these cords and there are barbs on them at the opposite end of the sender.

All aka cord attachments are undesirable. They emanate to and from people through weakness in their auric field caused by negative feelings of insecurity, anger, fear, etc. These connections are an energy drain for the one being corded. Most people attach cords from a sub-conscious level and are unaware of it. There are those however, who do it consciously for the purpose of manipulating thoughts or feelings of the one they cord—they are usually familiar with some type of sorcery (from past or present lives).

If you have aka cords, you may feel various sensations in the body at the point of connection. These have been described as nausea, pain, twisting or pulling, or just a general lack of energy. If you ever had the feeling of being torqued at the thought of a particular person, you have one or more strong aka cords between you. Emotions travel through these cords, often creating a severe emotional reaction to a person or situation. You can have several cords from several people at the same time. You can have cords attached with loved ones as well as enemies.

The most important thing you can do for a relationship is to remove the aka cords. This will assist you in dealing with that person from a clear perspective, releasing the negative emotional entanglements. Love between people creates merging on a spirit/soul level, so the removal of aka cords does not sever the love aspect of a relationship in any way. In fact, it opens the opportunity to improve upon it.

You can use the following process as a general "looking" for any cord connections or to see if one particular person at a time is connected. Follow the same general procedures listed in the beginning of this chapter.

Removing Aka Cords

Begin with the Breath of Ha (complete that process)

In your mind, you can create a darkened theatre with a stage and spotlights. You can also do this in your own Private Sanctuary (see Toolbox). Place yourself on the stage and call upon Divine Guidance to shine a large spotlight upon you. Ask your inner child (kino aka) to assist. As you stand in the center you will see that the inside of the shaft of light facing you is completely mirrored. You now have psychic visual access to your whole body.

Now examine your entire body and see where cords of any thickness are sticking out and to whom they are attached. The cords will be dark shades of various colors depending on the predominant emotion running through them. Your spotlight may be full of people—some may be in the darkness at a distance. Locate the thickest cord and see who is at the other end. Do this by pulling the cord toward you, into the center of your light. See both of you standing on the stage in the same spotlight. Tell the corded one, in a calm compassionate tone to request support from their own Divine Source. You are now going to move them out of your energy field and into their own spotlight, located well away from yours.

Tell them you do not want this kind of connection and you are going to remove the cord from yourself. Ask your Guidance to mentally hand you the appropriate tool that is to be used to remove the cord. It will mentally appear in your hand. Ask your body to prepare for the severing. You may feel various physical or emotional sensations as you cut the cord. Do not be alarmed. Sensations are a verification of how strong some connections can be. Look for any roots or tendrils still inside and remove them, or ask your guides for assistance. Roots denote a past life connection.

Notice the reaction of the other person but don't allow it to disturb your process. They may be angry, sad or weakened. This release is as good for their healing, as it is for your own. We must all learn to connect to our own Divine Source for life force energy and not siphon it from others through fear, anger or desire. Ask your Guidance provide healing energy to the area. You can also put your strongest hand over the area and fill it with Light.

When all the "surgery" is complete give thanks to all who assisted you. Take your time in resuming daily activities. You may find you need to rest and drink water.

A Little More Info

Some of the tools that are given are quite interesting and usually very symbolic. One woman, corded by an abusive husband, was handed an axe to sever a huge cord. Another was given an abalone shell knife. Laser wands, blow torches, chain saws, swords, holy water, screwdrivers and simply pulling cords out by hand are just a few of the methods that have been used.

Sometimes people see a hole where the cord has been. A method I use to repair and heal this condition when guiding someone through this process is to suggest they take a handful (or bucketful) of crystals, gems, flowers or colored light, liquid or gel and put it into the hole. If you prefer another substance, that is fine. You know what you need for the situation. Indeed, the greatest tool for healing is the creative imagination. I encourage you to trust your own intuitive knowing in all of these processes. Too many people have allowed their natural creative function to be severely suppressed. When in doubt, ask your higher self (makua keahu) to assist you. Allow yourself to rest after this process, and to release any emotions that come up.

To complete the release you can send the other person love from your heart center by directing a rose-pink ray of love to their heart. This eases the separation, which will be felt by the person as you sever the cords. They may even contact you shortly after the process. There is a difference between having your life force energy taken from you through cord attachments, and giving it freely, from your own Source. When we give, we are continuously replenished.

It is best to sever any aka cords before moving to the next Ho'oponopono Process, which is for all levels of your being—mental, spiritual and physical (they are all connected).

Ho'oponopono—General Questionnaire and Process

The first time you do this process between yourself and others, you can begin with the folowing general questionnaire. In this way you can cover past situations up to present day. In cases where there is a strong relationship with a person, place or thing, it is best to do a separate process specifically on this relationship.

Be sure you allow plenty of time without outside distractions because you will be processing as you write. Go back as far in time as needed, including any past-life information you are aware of. Ask your kino aka to give you information from your sub-conscious records and write down WHATEVER comes to mind. The manifestations of this process can be immediate or eventual. The POWER is in the WORD and the INTENT of the individual. I suggest doing this at night as it has more psychological impact.

This questionnaire can be expanded, by going through photo albums, if you have them. It can also be fun if you use your sense of humor. Doing it with a group can be a great supportive therapy as the old stuff is remembered, shared and released. The questions on the list are stated, one at a time, and the answers are written on paper. After the questionnaire and process are finished you can do a ceremony of completion. Create your own, whatever feels right to you, allowing your feelings to guide you. It can be elaborate or simple. The ceremony I use is to gather all the questionnaire papers from everyone and place them in a container. We all go outside to the patio and ceremonially burn each one, while observing the beautiful transmuting flames of the fire. This is always more dramatic in the dark atmosphere of night

You will find as you begin to cleanse away contrary experiences of the past, you will feel lighter. This process can be used whenever you feel the need. As you clear away the situations you are conscious of, others will float to the surface. You will then be able to process them as they arise. This can assist you in preventing overload.

The Questionnaire

(NARRATE): Write answers down as they come, even if you have passed the current category. It doesn't matter if they are in order. No one else has to see your papers. You can share them or keep them to yourself. Include in all your answers all people (or animals) who are deceased.

1. Your present full name.

2. Your present spouse (if any), including in-laws.

3. Your past spouse (if any), including past in-laws.

4. Any live-in mates, present or past.

5. Your parents: natural, step, or adopted.

6. Your grandparents and great-grandparents (any you recall).

7. Your children, grandchildren, etc: natural, step or adopted.

8. Your brothers/sisters: natural, step or adopted.

9. Your nephews, nieces, uncles, aunts and cousins (any you recall).

10. Other intimate friends and associates (individual or group).

11. Your occupations, employers, associates, etc.

12. Any individual or group you feel is contrary to you or your beliefs.

13. Any material objects, properties or locations (past or present).

14. Miscellaneous (any other not included above).

Fold or twist all papers, gather together in a circle (standing or sitting), place the papers in a pile in the center. Now recite the Ho'oponopono Process between the self and all that is listed on the papers. This can be done by one person, on behalf of all, or all can recite together.

The Ho'oponopono Process

1. The Breath of Ha (complete that process)

2. (NARRATE FROM THIS POINT ON): "Divine Creator and all Divine Beings who assist me, I request your attention to witness and to bless this Ho'oponopono Process."

3. (IF YOU WISH TO DO THE COMPLETE PROCESS BETWEEN YOURSELF AND YOUR INNER FAMILY, SEE THE PREVIOUS HO'OPONOPONO PROCESS. ONCE YOU ARE FAMILIAR WITH IT, YOU MAY SIMPLY RECITE THE FOLLOWING):

    "Makua keahu and kino aka, I now invoke the entire Ho'oponopono Process between myself and my inner family. It is done!"

4. "I (state your name), now wish to do a Ho'oponopono between myself and (whomever/whatever, or all listed on questionnaire), to correct, cleanse and release all disharmonious thoughts, words, actions and deeds from the beginning of creation to the present. I humbly ask for and give to them complete forgiveness. I request that all contrary karmic ties be transmuted into Pure Light including all objects, locations and situations involved."

5. TO AFFIRM—(IF NARRATOR IS RECITING, HAVE ALL RECITE EACH LINEOF PRAYER AFTER YOU).

    (Ancient Hawaiian prayer)
    "I AM THE I"
    I come forth from the void into Light,
    I am the breath that nurtures Life.
    I am that emptiness, that hollowness beyond all consciousness,
    The I, the Id, the All.
    I draw my bow of rainbows across the waters,
    The continuum, of minds with matters.
    I am the incoming and outgoing of breath,
    The invisible, untouchable breeze,
    The undefinable atom of creation…I AM THE I.

6. I now acknowledge and give thanks to all who are present, of all time/space dimensions, of all vibrations. We are free…and it is done!

7. TO CLEAR: At this time, you bathe in water as a final cleansing. This can be done actually, in any body of water or symbolically, by sprinkling water or visualizing water flowing over you. Create this in any form that feels right to you. The papers can be gathered and disposed of in the final ceremony of your choice.

Clearing & Blessing for House & Land

I created this ceremony incorporating a form of Ho'oponopono, prayers from ancient Hawaiian ceremonies, and direction from my Spirit Guides. I am sharing this with you, for your personal use. However, I caution anyone who has destructive haunting activity, to consult a practitioner for assistance.

The tools that are used are: a bowl made from a natural substance (mine is Koa wood), water with natural salt dissolved in it or ocean water, the leaves or a sprig of a plant that is special to you or your culture, particularly if it is growing on the land to be cleared (I use Ti leaf), and an offering of food, flowers or any other item you feel is appropriate. Place the offering in the center of the circle of participants.

The permission of all owners and/or tenants is necessary and they should be present if possible. Everyone who wishes to can participate, each holding a leaf. A leaf should be added for each absent person involved. Those who are fearful should be allowed to abstain by removing themselves from the property—the ceremony can be led by one person. This process should be done with reverence and clear intent. All who are present should do their own Ho'oponopono process first.

I usually read the entire ceremony from my book, even though I have done clearing and blessing processes for many years. This allows for the focus to be maintained on the ceremony, especially helpful when strong energy activity is moving through you or around you. This strong activity can be interference or simply a large astral crowd making an exit. Either way, you must continue the process until completion. Sometimes this requires your own strong resistance to fear. Know that if you have prepared properly, you are protected. It is simply a matter of holding strong in your Faith and your Intent.

The ancient Hawaiian prayers used in this process are taken from the book *Na Pule Kahiko, Ancient Hawaiian Prayers,* by June Gutmanis (see Bibliography) printed in both Hawaiian and English. I have edited and condensed them from the original writing. You can substitute them with other appropriate prayers.

(ALL GATHER IN A CIRCLE, IN OR OUT OF DOORS)

1. (NARRATE): "Let us first do the Breath of Ha" (complete that process)

"We call upon Divine Creator, the Aumakuas, the Elders and Ancestors of this land—We call upon Archangel Michael—We call upon the Guardians of the land, the sea and the sky—the East, the South, the West and the North. We acknowledge you, and all Great Spirits of all time/space, dimensions and frequencies. We humbly request of you to witness and to bless this ceremony!

We (each state your name), our families and ancestors, wish to do a Ho'oponopono of these premises and all matter, animate or inanimate in all time/space, dimensions and frequencies. If there are any discarnate earthbound spirits and/or negative vibrations within, on, or around us, we humbly ask for forgiveness on their behalf and ask that they be released into Divine Light, as they release us. We Are All Set Free! It Is Done!"

2. (TAKE ALL THE LEAVES, HOLD THEM TOGETHER, DIP THEM IN THE SALT WATER, AND SPRAY IN THE FOUR CARDINAL DIRECTIONS OF EAST, SOUTH, WEST AND NORTH, DIPPING THE LEAVES EACH TIME).

3. (RECITE THE FOLLOWING PRAYER—PLEASE NOTE: THE FIRST LINE VARIES, DEPENDING ON THE CIRCUMSTANCES. READ ONLY THE ONE THAT APPLIES TO YOUR SITUATION).

    A. (NEW BUILDING) "We cut the navel cord (pico) of this place."

    B. (EXISTING BUILDING) "This building stands, this building is solid."

    C. (LAND) "This land is stable, this land is solid."

    (CONTINUE RECITING PRAYER):
    "At the time of the dark to the time of the light,
    At the time of the partial blackness,
    At the time of the receding sea,
    At the time of the arrival of the sea,
    Above and below.
    At the time that has come to an end,
    It is time to free this place of kapu.
    Live—give life to the people,
    Give life to the land

Divine Creator,
Here is the offering.
Come into this place,
Into the heart and spirit of this place.
A place to revive life, a place to extend life.
Grant life to a sick one who enters this place of life,
A person in trouble who enters this place,
A person near death who enters this place.
Grant life to all who are present, your descendants in this world,
Grant life to their spouses and to their children and to their elders,
Grant life to those who dwell herein, that they may prosper.
That the guest who enters here may have health,
That the lord of the land may have health,
That the chiefs may have long life.
May there be well-being in this earthly life.
Profound kapu—profound be the removal of the kapu
It is free of kapu!"

4. NARRATE: "I now request of all discarnates who have chosen to stay with this land—please be understanding of those who are still embodied. Be forgiving of our ignorance and our fear about your world. In return, those of us who are embodied visitors or caretakers of this place, will be respectful of you, the buildings, the stones, the flora, the fauna and the land…let there be peace and harmony between us all."

5. (GATHER ALL THE LEAVES AND TACK THEM AT THE MAIN ENTRANCE OF THE BUILDING OR LAND).

6. (RECITE:) This final prayer continues in perpetuation:

"O guardians of these people, from remote antiquity,
Watch over this place
From top to bottom; from one corner to the other;
From East to West, the North to the South;
From the mountains to the sea, from the inside to the outside.
Watch over and protect it; ward off all that may trouble this place.
By The People, the prayer is freed!"

Take the remaining water and go through the building, pouring a small amount down each drain (this includes toilets). This is done to protect any opening into the earth. If you are blessing land only, the first choice is to pour it into a body of water. If none is available, pour in onto a bare patch of earth or rock.

Take the offering to a chosen spot outside, to be left. When the leaves at the entrance turn brown, they, along with any flower or food offering, can be removed and buried. Give thanks to all Divine Beings you have called upon.

Additional Tools

I would like to share some other tools that I have created or collected from other sources. These tools can enhance the basic processes described. They can be used separately or in combination, incorporated into other practices of your own. We have been referred to as eclectic practitioners. We encourage incorporation of all tools that embody the Universal Principles. The power of the tools is in the clarity of focused intent. Keep it simple.

Personal Divination

In addition to the tools in this book, I encourage you to explore the many tools available for personal divination. These tools can be very helpful to enhance and clarify communication with our Inner Family and Divine Guidance. You can also create your own objects or forms of divination.

Some examples of items available are: Tarot Cards (many different styles), Rune Stones, I Ching, Medicine Cards, Sacred Path Cards, the Transformation kit, Inner Child Cards, throwing bones or shells, reading tea leaves and many others. Choose those that feel right for you. Use discernment as you would with any other material. Personal preparation instructions come with most of these tools. It is important that you are in a mode of readynes and preparedness before beginning, as described at beginning of this chapter. These tools can bring valuable insight drawn to you from within yourself, that part of you that has access to your personal Divine Guidance. These tools can have strong energy but have no willful power in and of themselves: their empowerment comes from the Self.

I gratefully acknowledge the original creators of the following tools. I will state their names as known or I will state the name of the person who introduced them to me. Some of the tools came from my own Guidance team, thank you.

Remember to begin each process with the Breath of Ha and Ho'oponopono between your three selves and between yourself and others when it is appropriate.

The Breath Of Blue And Gold

Shared by: Ralph and Lois Mitchell

The purpose of this exercise is to balance your electromagnetic polarity. This stabilizes the emotional, mental and physical bodies. It increases your energy and your connection to your Higher Self. It is a quick, powerful way of centering yourself. This is good to use whenever you feel pressured, depressed, angry or just plain tired.

Sit or stand in a comfortable position, keeping your back straight, so the energy has a clear pathway.

Imagine a pool of golden light above your head and a pool of sapphire blue light beneath your body (feet or buttocks).

As you inhale, pull the golden light down through your crown, sweeping it through your body and down into the earth.

As you exhale, pull the sapphire blue light up through your body, sweeping it through your body and out the top of your head.

Do this sequence of breathing 7 times. Breathe at your own pace. The deeper the breath, the more extensive the effect.

The Light Invocation

Shared by: DaEl Walker

The words in this invocation were chosen and tested with energy sensitive equipment. This specific combination of words was found to have maximum empowerment. This invocation raises your vibratory rate and increases the Light Energy in your auric field dramatically, which also increases the Light in your immediate environment. Mr. Walker invites all to share this invocation for whatever purpose; ceremonies, correspondence, business cards, etc. His only request is that we share it EXACTLY as it was originally written.

Repeat the invocation 3 times. It is most powerful when said aloud.

I INVOKE THE LIGHT OF THE CHRIST WITHIN
I AM A CLEAR AND PERFECT CHANNEL
LIGHT IS MY GUIDE.

This can be used whenever you feel a need for protection, upliftment or healing. It enhances the immune system. You can use a dowsing rod to see the difference in your aura before and after.

The Golden Egg

Shared by Bobby Lopes and Jeri
This etheric energy egg is for protection.
Mentally surround yourself and your outer auric field with Divine White Light in
the shape of an egg. Hold this thought or picture in your mind until it is full and
warm. If you wish, you can recite the Light Invocation to intensify this process.
Call upon Archangel Michael to cover the entire outer shell of the egg with his
sapphire blue ray of protection.
Seal the outer blue layer with a layer of pure gold glitter. Gold protects from cosmic interference.
This egg can be invoked whenever you feel the need for protection on a physical
or nonphysical level. You can also invoke it to extend around a vehicle or vessel
you are in.
Give thanks to Archangel Michael for his assistance.

A Private Sanctuary

Shared by: Jeri
Everyone needs private alone time, although for some it is very difficult to obtain.
The sanctuary I will describe can be created by anyone. It is created by thought
and its location is on the inner planes of your mind. It can never be visited by
anyone without your permission. You create every aspect of it to your liking. You
can use it for rest, healing, problem solving, communication with other people
and their inner child, or any other purpose you wish. I was introduced to a similar process when I attended the PSI Basic seminar, created by Thomas Willhite
(now deceased), many years ago.
To create your sanctuary, sit or lie quietly and use any relaxation method that works
for you, such as soothing music or nature sounds. When you are completely
relaxed, you will be able to visualize. Refer to techniques at beginning of this chapter.

To Begin
First create the room or place for your inner sanctuary. Indoors or outdoors, create
an environment that is perfect for you. There are some items that will be useful:

1.   A viewing screen of any type

2.   A communication center of any type

3. A place for rest

4. A place and any equipment for healing

5. A place or object to access all knowledge

6. A place to receive and visit with guests

7. A place or object to clear your vibrations as you enter and as you leave

Create each part as you desire. You may even find that you change some of it later. You can alter your sanctuary until it is perfect for you. Trust that you have the ability to mentally create any of the equipment you may need. When it is complete request Divine Blessing and protection from your personal Divine Guidance.

As an example, I will share some of my sanctuary decor. It is a large room, carpeted with beautiful Persian carpet. Comfortable furniture, a large movie screen with violet velvet drapes, an entire wall of books with a ladder that rolls back and forth. For healing, I use glass chambers with gemstone tables. For guests, there is a garden entrance and lounge area. At the entrance/exit is a floating pyramid that emits Divine Light for cleansing. This round room is at the top of a hill overlooking an ocean, with steps down to the water. I travel to and from there on a flying Persian carpet (with fringe).

Allow your creative imagination to take over and en-joy!

Personal Altar (Vortex)

Shared by: Jeri

Ceremony or ritual can be a very powerful way to acknowledge a specific event, a season in our life cycles or for ongoing prayer work. The repetition of any given process is what empowers it. Each time it is performed with strong intent, energy is added to the meaning. An example of this is the Ho'oponopono Process, a very ancient and sacred ritual, which has been used by so many over the centuries that the word itself is a very powerful catalyst for the basic procedure.

This same principle applies to the location of a ceremony. Each time a ceremony is repeated with strong intent at the same location, the energy of the ceremony is imprinted upon the site. When a site is designated for a specific process and continually used for that process, it becomes a vortex for that process. These locations can be any size. Some names for them are altars, shrines, sacred sites or heiaus (Hawaiian).

Many followers of orthodox religions have personal altars in their homes. The heiaus of Hawaii were usually formed with stones. They were used for many purposes, some of which were/are: requesting rain control, insuring crops, good fishing, honoring deities, seasonal ritual and healing. All were and still are considered sacred places of worship. Many sites are still preserved and most of them still contain the energy of past and/or present ceremonies. These types of altars are created in sacred ceremony and are for the purpose of invoking a specific energy to make contact with the Divine Spirit beings that assist humans with the issues of survival on the earthly plane—like a telephone booth connected to heaven.

There are other types of personal altars that people use even though they may not realize they have created them. A vanity table is an example, or a workbench and tools in the garage. Perhaps a sewing or craft center is in a specific place in the home, or a drawing board. A little offering or prayer may enhance production there.

Creating a personal altar can be fun and it is easy. Pick a spot on the floor or the top of a table, box or other object. You can put any items on it that are appropriate for your purpose. You can have it indoors or outdoors, in your home or in some other favorite spot that is not used for anything else. Be creative as you adorn it. Then begin to create its purpose with a statement of your intent in a ceremonial manner. You can change the adornment as you wish, but enter your intent into each new item added. Make offerings to your Divine Guidance team as a gesture of gratitude. Most like flowers and other fragrant things (please, no bribery or offerings of "first born" children).

You can create a personal multi-purpose altar or one with singular focus. Use it to celebrate your achievements and empower them. Use it for celebrating the seasons or to mark/celebrate births and deaths in your circle as rites of passage. Beware of becoming attached to the objects on your altar—you are the one with the power. Fill those items with your intention with love and for the highest good for all in accordance with the "law of right action."

In my living room I use a small table as a group altar for clearing negative energy or situations (mahiki), and healing. The altar has candles of different colors, a variety of incense, some dry herbs and other personal objects, which change from time to time, depending on the work we are doing. Often, other people place objects there for processing—one client placed a document from a pending court case, another; the papers from a new business he was creating.

Using an altar is not really necessary to do prayer or energy work. We are Divine self-contained creators ourselves. However, being human, we do respond to physical visual props. An altar and the objects on it are simply an aid for focus and additional symbolic energy. The power is in the intent and the reinforcement of that intent.

Create your own processes or choose those that are suitable to your needs and beliefs. Each time you repeat your intention, you empower it. This is true of all of our thoughts and words.

Magic Dowsing Rod

Shared by DaEl Walker

During a crystal workshop given in 1987 by DaEl Walker, we were shown how to make our own dowsing rod out of a wire coat hanger and a plastic straw. It has been a great tool to demonstrate the effects of thoughts, crystals and other items on our personal energy fields.

SUPPLIES: a wire coat hanger and a plastic straw

TOOLS: wire cutters and needle nose pliers

TO MAKE: Unwind the hanger at the neck. Measure 12 inches from one bent corner along the center and cut. Open bent corner until the hanger forms an L. Measure up the remaining side 4 1/2 inches and cut. Measure 4 inches of plastic straw and cut it cleanly. Slide straw onto small section of wire, this is your handle. With tip of pliers, bend the tip of the handle wire under—leaving space for the straw to roll around freely on the wire handle. Grasp the straw-covered handle [shortest wire] gently and swing the long wire to be sure it rotates freely over your fist.

The Magic Show

TO USE: Stand ten or more feet away from the person or thing you wish to measure. Grasp the handle of the rod while pointing the long end at the person. Slowly, steadily walk toward them until the long wire moves to either side, then stop. This is the edge of the energy field.

When measuring the effects of an object or substance, have the person hold it near the center stomach area (solar plexus). Measure the person's aura in normal state before experimenting. That would usually be about 2 to 3 feet. Then you can do a simple experiment, as follows:

Use a small plain quartz crystal that has been washed with soap and water. The first step is to touch it to your forehead and think the word "ouch"—then hand it to a volunteer to hold in their hand at their solar plexus. Then from about 10 feet away, start walking toward them, slowly, with the dowser in your hand, pointing straight forward. When the wire moves to the side, STOP! That is the edge of their auric field. It will probably be rather close to them, as the thought of ouch will weaken them. Tell them what the word was.

Then, take the crystal from them and blow it clear with your breath. Now, touch it to your forehead and think the word "love"—then hand it to the same volunteer to hold at their solar plexus. Then go about 10 to 20 feet away from them and start walking toward them, slowly, with the wire pointed straight at them. When the wire moves to the side, Stop, again. You will probably be quite a distance from them this time—their aura will be strengthened by love—as are all things. A simple lesson on good and bad thoughts, and how powerful they really are.

A String To The Past

Shared by Jeri

There are times when situations from our past, of this life or past lives, create issues that we need to address in the present. This process is a simple method of retrieving memory. Some of you may require hypnosis if you are dealing with a deeply buried trauma. If that is the case, I suggest you seek a practitioner to assist you. Let us begin by relaxing your mind and body, sit quietly on the floor or bed. A darkened room may be a more conducive atmosphere but it is not essential.

Picture in your mind, a beautiful lighted ball of string. If you prefer yarn or thicker string, that is fine too. Make it any color you wish, or even multi-colored. See it as the size of a large grapefruit. Hold it or roll it around in your two hands, firmly. As you do this, you are imprinting all of your memory, from all lifetimes into it.

Tie the loose end of the string to any part of your body, a toe, a finger, around your waist. Now, think of what information you wish to have, ask Guidance and your inner child to assist you, and state your request. And when you are ready, mentally, throw the ball over your shoulder with force. Then, turn around and face the direction you threw the ball. You will now be facing in the opposite direction you were before—your past, behind you. You have a little time to turn, so you don't need to do it too quickly. The ball never runs out of string so no time or distance is too great.

Take a deep breath and relax and wait for the information to come back to you. This can be in the form of pictures, or words or just a knowing or feeling. It doesn't matter. The ball may return with it, or it simply may reappear in your hands when the answer is complete.

Practice this process a few times on something easy, like recalling a birthday party or something similar, with no trauma attached. The more you use the tool the easier it will become. Give thanks for the assistance.

Measure of Forgiveness

Shared by Jeri

Forgiveness is the key to healing the pain and anger from our hearts. Fear is the underlying original cause of all negative feelings. Doubt and disconnection from Spirit is behind all fear. Sometimes it is difficult to begin the process of forgiveness, especially when the pain or anger is very deep or longstanding.

I was working with a native Hawaiian client on forgiveness when my Hawaiian Spirit Guide presented this process. It entails offering food in increasing amounts, as the measure of forgiveness that you are willing to give, on a daily basis.

Using food was very appropriate for this client because of the cultural importance placed on the growing and gathering of food, which is still very strong in Hawaii today. My client grew most of the food he used. For all of us, food is sustenance and nurturing, and a meal is at the center of many of our activities. To many, dessert is a little extra love, or at least an extra treat.

I suggest you work with one situation (or person) at a time in your forgiveness process. You can actually give the offering to the person or, more often, place it in a chosen spot for this process. This is one way you can use an altar.

Begin by choosing a food that is the size of the amount of forgiveness you are willing to start with. In the case of my client, I asked him if he could manage to give even one grain of rice. He agreed, and that was his first offering.

This begins the process within your heart. Each day, make the food item a little larger. It doesn't matter how long it takes. In five days my client was offering a very large squash. The following day he was able to give complete forgiveness by saying it from his heart.

At this point you can make a final offering of a personal gift or flowers to the person or on the altar. In my client's case, the person he needed to forgive had been dead for several years but the continued anger was causing sleep disturbances and health problems for him.

Anger can cripple or kill the one who carries it if it is not processed in a productive way and released. Use this and any of the other tools in this book to assist you in resolving your feelings.

Anger Pillow

Shared by: Jeri

As a family abuse counselor, I began to use this tool with abused children, many of whom, often fight with other children. It is very beneficial in releasing stored anger, hatred, pain and frustration, for people of ALL ages.

I encourage you to make your own pillow, but it is not absolutely necessary. It needs to be large enough to cover your whole face and thick enough to muffle loud yelling or crying.

If you want to make your own, choose whatever fabric would feel good on your face, in whatever colors of solid or print you feel drawn to. Perhaps a color or print that looks like anger. Use materials that are washable. Decide the measurements and allow for the seams. Then choose stuffing. Old clothes, towels or blankets can be used. Or you can simply recover an old or new pillow. When it is finished, ask you spirit guides to fill it full of pure Light. This will transmute the feelings automatically so they don't spill out to anyone else or begin to accumulate in your space.

I suggest that you do not use this pillow for any other purpose. You can carry it with you while awake, but I encourage you keep it away from you when you sleep. And do not let anyone else use it, they should make their own. You will need to clear it when you feel the need by washing it or running cold water over it.

This pillow can be used to scream, cry or swear into. Be as loud as you can and say exactly what you feel. Whatever is said into the anger pillow is not to be criticized by anyone! This is your own personal ranting and raving. RELEASE…and Let it go!

Give It A Form

Shared by Suzanne Joyce and Jeri

Feelings are sometimes difficult to specifically identify, especially when we are right in the middle of an overload. Often, there is a combination of feelings or emotions tangled up together. I feel we can release the contrary or negative ones easier if we give them a form. This can be done whether we can identify them or not.

If you feel the urge to cry or vent anger, do this first to release the excess. You can use the Anger Pillow (above) first to assist this release. Afterward, you can do the following process.

You can ask a friend to coach you if they are able to remain neutral and not criticize. Take the strongest feelings first. If you can separate them do this process with each, one at a time—if not, then process them together.

Sit or lie down in a comfortable position. Request the assistance of your personal Divine Guidance. Take several deep breaths to center your focus. If you are feeling any pain or discomfort somewhere in your physical body, focus on that area. The feelings manifest most often in the heart or stomach areas.

Now, give a form to your feeling(s). Allow yourself to create the form, the size and the color. Example: anger might look like a big red blob or lightning bolts, etc. Fear might be a black monster of some sort. We each have our own symbolic code. Allow the picture or thought of the form to come in.

Once the form(s) appear, ask your Divine Guidance to assist you in removing the form from wherever it appears, inside or outside your body. Request that this energy and all that is connected to it be transmuted into Pure Light. This prevents these contrary feelings from affecting anyone around you as they are released. Nothing is ever destroyed, it can only be changed into other forms of energy—ideally, higher vibrations. You may even see one of your guides come and take it away for you.

As the form is being removed, listen to your Divine Guidance for any instructions they may be giving you for this process. When you have completed the process, give thanks to your Guidance. Allow yourself time to rest and reflect.

Worry Time

Shared by: Jeri

A great deal of time in our lives is wasted on worrying. It is wasted time because worry never solves anything but usually exaggerates the situation and always brings stress to the body, mind and spirit, and places us into a mode of depression. It is human nature to worry, however, and I feel we can do it in a more productive, less destructive way. You can call it a meditation in depression.

This process can be done before your daily meditation or prayer time. Create a time when you will be undisturbed. Have paper and writing/drawing tools. Include "worry beads" or any other object you may need to facilitate your session. Use a timer so you will not go over your limit. Decide how much time you need but take no more than 30 minutes a day! You can ask your inner child to join you, if they wish.

When you begin, make a list of all the things that you are worried about, in priority. Then choose one at a time, starting with your smallest worry. This will get you into practice for the big ones at the top of your list.

To begin: pure, concentrated, uninterrupted worrying. The rules are as follows:

1.   You must do nothing but worry.

2. You must think of nothing else but your worries.

3. You must do this process daily, until you have no more worries.

4. You are only allowed to worry during your allotted time.

When your Worry Time is finished, I suggest you do some deep breathing to relax, or take a bath or shower. You can write down any solutions that may have occurred to you.

If any worries come up at other times during your day, you may NOT worry about them—you can write them on your Worry List and include them in your next session. If you find yourself slipping, you MUST think or do something that will make you laugh. Now, do try to enjoy the twenty-three and one half hours you have left!

The Love Letter

Shared by: Dona Lock and Norma Marie
We began using this version (as was shared with us) of the Love Letter in 1985. The contributors received it during a workshop given by Dr. Barbara De Angelis and John Grey. The original version is in a teaching manual they developed in 1982 for the Los Angeles Personal Growth Center and was included in Dr. De Angelis' book, titled *How to Make Love All the Time*, Dell Publishing 1987 (see Bibliography).

This is one of the most powerful tools available to use for a personal release. I call it emotional archeology, moving through the layers of buried feelings, thoughts or attitude patterns of the emotional body, releasing them, transmuting them to love and understanding and self-empowerment. This can be an intensive aid to the Aka Cord and Ho'oponopono Processes. I suggest you cut aka cords before doing the Love Letter, then completion after the Letter by doing the Ho'oponopono Process.

The Love Letter is to be written to the self or to anyone you have negative feelings about. I suggest you begin with your parents, addressing each one separately, even if you do not think you have any friction with them. There is always a little stuff, it comes with the job as parents. Then proceed to any other strong relationships where there was or is friction. If you are in a crisis situation with a current relationship, you can begin with that person(s).

This process can also be done on a cassette tape. The rules are important, but simple:

1. Respond to one line at a time until you are empty of reply.

2. Don't hold back—swear, draw pictures, but put all your feelings on the paper/cassette.

3. When complete, the letter must be read aloud to you by someone you trust, or by yourself while standing in front of a mirror. If you taped your letter, play it back.

4. No comments are to be made by the person reading it back to you.

5. You must respond to the lines in order and you must finish all seven lines for this process to be complete.

6. DON'T mail the letter to the person you write to. You can read it to them, but ONLY if they know the rules and they have the right to reply in the Love Letter format. It is not necessary to share this letter directly with the person you write it to. They will receive it on the Spirit level and you may be pleasantly surprised at their reaction. Don't be concerned, however, THIS PROCESS IS FOR YOU!

The letter may take you two hours or two days—it doesn't matter. You may need to stop and cry or yell. The Anger Pillow is good for this, or take a short walk in between the lines. Just do it! This process is like peeling an emotional onion, one layer at a time, starting with the top layer and going back to the initial desires of the relationship. Some relationships can be healed and re-routed, others simply need to be released. This process is a healing for either choice.

After you are finished with the whole process, you can ceremonially burn the Letter, transmuting all the negative feelings into a better understanding. This brings you more into balance where you are able to express your true feelings. In long-standing relationships (parents, children, mates) you may find that you want to write other letters in the future as you move into new levels with these relationships or new ones.

The format is as follows:

1. I AM ANGRY OR BLAME.................because

2. I AM SAD OR HURT....................because

3. I AM AFRAID........................because

4. I FEEL GUILTY OR RESPONSIBLE.........because

5. I UNDERSTAND AND FORGIVE

6. I LOVE

7. I WANT

The Planetary Circle of Light

Shared by: Julie Murphy, Lani Churchill and Jeri
This is Mothership Maui's offering to our planet Earth and her inhabitants. Each of us participates from wherever we are. The whales and dolphins love this one.
NOTE: Do each step in your own timing—breathe consciously, consistently. Allow yourself to tone, verbalize, and visualize (including color), as you are led by your own creative center.
PREPARATION: Do your own personal clearing process—then we suggest a Ho'oponopono between yourself and the planet Earth, and begin with the Breath of Ha.
INTENT: State your intent to offer your Love/Light to be used for the highest good of this planet and her inhabitants, in Right Action.
REQUEST: Call for assistance from your personal Divine Guidance, Planetary Guardians and All benevolent Beings of Divine Light, Archangel Michael, Divine Christ vibration or other to bless this process.

THE PROCESS:

1. Clear your auric field of any shadows, energies and entities.

2. Open your heart center—expand the pure love vibration from there.

3. Connect your inner family with a gold-white triangle of pure Light.

4. Create another triangle of Rainbow Light within it, forming a six-pointed star.

5. Create a circle of gold-white Light surrounding the star. Merge with Divine Source by placing yourself into a shaft of Rainbow Light, which is open at the top to Source, and at the bottom to the earth.

6. Request a blanket or corona of the sapphire-blue light of Archangel Michael to cover and protect your star creation.

7. Expand your aura slowly and carefully, as you intensify its luminosity.

8. Slowly, draw Rainbow Light from your Star-self (higher self), down through the shaft into the earth and through to the other side, out and around the earth in a complete circle, back to your Star-self. Feel when it is complete. Then reverse this process, drawing Rainbow Light up through the shaft, out the crown to the Star-self, then circling the earth, back to the Star-self, and down into the center of the earth. There, see the Light expanding and being received into the planetary network of Light, expanding outward through the entire earthly aura. Feel when it is complete. This pattern holds strong for 24 hrs.

9. Acknowledge and give thanks to all the Beings of Light you requested to assist you…And it is done.

NOTE: Rest, center, replenish yourself and drink water afterwards.

In Service

There are many people who believe they have incarnated on Earth at this time especially to be of service to Earth and her inhabitants. If you feel that you have a specific mission of service, then you probably do.

I believe we are all here to learn how to be of higher service, to the self and humanity as a whole. This can begin when we choose to move into a state of GRACE. The state of Grace is an ever-present mode of Right Action (acting from love). It is available to anyone who chooses to move toward their highest purpose. It requires forgiveness, of the self and others for any supposed wrong-doing. The mode of forgiveness moves us into Loving the self and others, unconditionally.

Service vs. Sacrifice

There is a fine line between service and sacrifice. I believe this is the lesson for those who are motivated to serve others. The lesser level of serving is a need to "make everything right" or to "fix" what is wrong, motivated by fear of rejection or punishment. This pattern is usually caused by growing up in a dysfunctional environment that creates a suppression of self in order to cope with the dysfunction of others around them, usually the dysfunction of those in authority roles, such as parents or other caretakers.

As this pattern manifests in adulthood, the need to serve in this sacrificial mode continues, creating stress in the body, mind and spirit, and continuing a cycle of dysfunctional relationships with associates, mates and offspring. The recognition of negative emotional patterns can create an opportunity for discovery. Healing begins at the moment of "awareness." If the dysfunctional emotional pattern continues unresolved, it manifests in the physical body, which begins to give loud signals of discomfort or shutdown. This is a further opportunity to discover dysfunctional emotional patterns, which are the root cause for physical disease.

Higher Service

The higher, or positive level of service to self uplifts and enlightens the whole of humanity. Higher service to the self, is higher service to others. Higher service to others, is higher service to the self. They are the same.

The higher level of serving anyone, is to help someone help themselves. Support them on any path that encourages their healthy functional behavior. Be supportive in their joy or pain, as each mode serves an equally important purpose for growth. Be willing to share tools and information that may assist them as you acknowledge and respect "their" picture of reality without judgement. Anything else is interference, manipulation, or control—and this serves no one.

Lightworker—Loveworker

There have been many terms used to describe those who are in earthly service to a heavenly cause. Currently, the most commonly used is that of Lightworker. I suggest that the term Lightworker creates a very limited picture of those it refers to. I choose to use the term Loveworker. In my understanding, it refers to those who have expanded their awareness to the reality of Universal Oneness in all things—a realization that what each of us thinks and feels affects the whole. These people choose to serve humanity at large and can receive assistance from the higher spiritual realms for this purpose. The choice of serving the higher good can be made at any time, by anyone.

Who Are They?

I suggest that Loveworker means one who is consciously loving—one who works in/with Divine Light, in all aspects of their lives. Divine Light is Love/Wisdom. A Loveworker is one who has Love as their intent and Higher Wisdom as their guidance. That is all—it is that simple.

Those of Love are motivated toward higher service to others, thus serving the balanced higher self. Those without Love are motivated to serve the dysfunctional lesser self, at the expense of all involved. This is how you will know them! Many work in the service professions of medicine, nursing and other healing arts, some are in food service or entertainment. One who is of higher service is one who likes and cares for or about people and themselves.

Making a conscious decision to move into the state of "Grace," empowers the Love/Light you already carry. It is a powerful opportunity to balance dysfunctional karmic patterns, thus being of service to the self and to all.

We have a lot of help from the Love/Light Beings of the higher realms, available to any who requests assistance. This guidance can come through your higher self (makua keahu), and from your Divine Guidance team.

I believe that "parenting" is the ultimate, the highest class on this planet. I believe parenting is the highest sacred role one can choose. It is an honor to be responsible for the formation of a person. I pray more parents realize this.

We Can Begin Now

We can all be of service to others while healing our selves. To serve the higher good IS our healing. To be of service is first to be true to the self by expressing your truth, with discernment and understanding. Love and care for the self. Discipline the self with focus. Then expand this to your family or household, then to the community and so on. As if you were a pebble of Light dropped into the center of a pond and the ripple of your presence radiates.

Do what brings you Joy, whether at work or at play. Learn to understand the dysfunctional aspects of your existence and how they serve your growth. Choose tools to assist you in healing contrary emotional patterns that do not serve your higher good so you can bring balance to your body, mind and spirit. Begin to clear your heart of pain, anger and fear. Begin to put your house and your affairs in order. Begin to heal your past through understanding, bringing Light into your present, so you can embrace your future with Love. Then, share this with others. As you make a conscious choice to move into a state of Grace—the ways and means will follow.

What is Love?

True Love, is unconditional—no strings (aka cords) attached, no fine print at the bottom of a contract, no expectation of "reward," here or "in heaven." The basic ingredients of love are: compassion, respect, kindness, courtesy, caring, forgiveness, etc. If these are not present, it is not love—it is something less. There are degrees and different types of Love: sexual, parent/child, siblings, friends, etc. Another type is Agape: unselfish love for humanity and all life.

It is often difficult to discern actual love within ourselves, or in others. I feel this discernment can be facilitated, if we remember those important basic ingredients, they are always the same. Love Enlightens. Love Heals. Love simply Feels Good to give and to receive.

Remain impersonal as you serve others. Unconditional love is impersonal. Discern what is Right Action by observing the Law of Free Will and do nothing that will knowingly bring harm to the self or another.

Connect to your Source. Use tools that assist you in connecting your inner selves. Use the methods that feel right to you, whether they are the ones in this book or others. Begin now, with a daily practice, to clear and center yourself. Offer your Love to the planetary network of Light by sending a pink ray of Love out over the Earth. You can do it right this minute!

Fill your heart with a soft rose-pink Love Light. Feel your heart expanding with a soft, warm, cozy, loving feeling. See the beautiful rose-pink light getting brighter from within you, expanding out into your whole body and outer aura. Feel the soft, tender, gentle love vibration all through your being. Bathe in this love until you feel warm.... see the pink light coming out of your heart...moving through the rooms...and out through the walls and the roof, expanding through the neighborhood and beyond, enveloping this planet...Thank you...it feels wonderful!

What About The Dark?

In the polarized physical and non-physical realms of existence there is a perception of positive and negative experience. Each experience is a necessary balance for the other. Each is for specific learning. The earth and lower astral realms are classrooms for the Good versus Evil, Light versus Dark scenarios. We are all here to experience this duality for the purpose of learning how to balance the positive and negative energies in ourselves and in our lives. Relationship is the catalyst for this lesson. The negative lessons leave the strongest impressions for humans because many believe in the "no pain—no gain" concept. Each of us has the ability to clear this limitation through understanding. This is the lesson!

The term "dark" is commonly used to refer to any thought or action that is contrary to Universal Principles. The word "evil" is used to refer to an extreme of contrary thought or action, which has the INTENT of causing harm to another.

In reality, there is Light (love/wisdom) in all things, including the dark, to a greater or lesser degree. Although the word dark is the most common terminology, a more accurate description of dark vs. light, is contrary vs. harmonious.

There are those who work with what I will term night or shadow energy, who have been labeled dark practitioners. This is a judgement based in fear and misunderstanding. Each of us works with dark, night or shadow energy every time we accept and move into the energy of anger or fear in order to transform it into harmony. Again, one's intent is the key. The seed of a flower must germinate in a dark damp place, before it emerges into the sunlight and blossoms into its beautiful ultimate form.

The Power of Light and Dark are two sides of the same coin. Power is just power, until it is utilized in one mode or another. Like electricity, it can bring energy into our lives for comfort and construction, or it can kill! How the power is used is our choice. INTENT is the key.

The contrary path is a more difficult experience, one of abuse and suffering. It is chosen by those whose beliefs are based in the idea of abuse and suffering, which they direct toward themselves and others. Each of us has had exposure to these patterns—they abound on this planet. ALL paths lead back to Creator. All are for exploration and experience in the polarity of good and evil. Judgement is not the issue, it is not for us to decide which path another should take.

Each of us has played all roles through one incarnation or another, just as a good actor chooses a variety of roles to expand and improve his skill. This duality is simply for the purpose of comparison in the denser levels of manifestation. The Law of Karma insures the continuing balance of Ultimate Right Action.

All contrary thoughts have a root of Fear. Ignorance opens the door and being fearful gives your power to contrary energies. The Light (wisdom, understanding, enlightenment) is your protection. Faith is the power for that Light. Light can dispel the shadows in the heart, mind and body. Follow the guidance of your higher self, heal your own guilt, pain and anger, and harm will not be drawn to you. As we transmute the energies of our own contrary emotional patterns and fill them with Divine Love and Light, we can accept Joy as a natural state of being. As we do this, we can move beyond our self-imposed limitations.

Discernment

I encourage all Loveworkers to gather and share information from a variety of sources. There are many good books, tapes and videos available. There are lots of tools for awakening the memory that we carry from our heritage, our past incarnations of this earthly realm and beyond. Some of the information being channeled into our world now is simply a catalyst to trigger our innate knowing and to release that knowledge for us to use in our lives. Some of what we carry is misinformation, formed from a lack of knowledge or misinterpretation at the time of the experience. Some material is intentional disinformation, which includes what is channeled through our news media regarding daily events that are changing our lives. A characteristic of disinformation is that it is often camouflaged with some truth and pleasant verbiage, to get it through our filters.

It is important that we use discernment with ALL the information we read, see, hear or feel. Give careful attention to any information that negates Choice or Free Will, encourages fear, or is only given with a high price tag. There are those who propose that we follow their leadership for salvation. There are those who seem to perform miracles of healing or other demonstrations of abilities or power. The common thread in these situations is the idea that the right answers are outside of our selves. Anything that intends to draw us away from our inner, Higher Guidance, is a lie!

Play in the Light

Light is a powerful thing, even the simple light of a household bulb. Here is an experiment you can do at home: Use a 100 watt bulb on a cord or a small lamp. Try to place it somewhere that will completely conceal ALL the light of the bulb, a room, a closet, a drawer, a box. Difficult, isn't it?

Love light is far more powerful than darkness, even in small doses—consider a smile. A smile is a wonderful way to share Light with others. There are many who are surrounded by darkness in their lives and a simple smile can ignite the Light they have buried deep inside. Another way to brighten the Light within each of us is to PLAY. Healthy, harmless play is a healing in itself. Encourage playing in your lives with your friends and family. Play games, play sports, play at whatever brings you Joy. Love Light is very powerful magic!

Everyone has at least a spark of Light in their heart. We are all children of God, Divine Creator (source). My simplified version of God is one huge central source of pure, powerful life-force energy. See it as a big sparkler, like the ones used on the 4th of July or Chinese New Year. As it is ignited, it throws off billions (it's really big!) of sparks. I see each of those sparks as a soul. Each spark is a piece of the original substance of the sparkler. The sparkler and its sparks never burn out...we are immortal.

Spirit Guides

All people have Spirit Guides who are available to help. Some people have Spirits who manipulate them, depending on one's capacity for Love, giving and receiving. Those who have chosen the path of Love have Guides from the higher spiritual realms and some have benevolent ancestors. Those who have chosen a darker path have less capacity for Love, and can be manipulated by Spirits who are self-serving. There are two general categories of influence, those of higher vibration: Higher Angelic beings, benevolent ancestors (Aumakua) and ascended human Spirits who are master teachers, and some species of benevolent extraterrestrials, who all serve the highest purpose for humanity—and those of lower vibration: Lower astral beings, elementals, malevolent human discarnates (including some ancestors), and ascended human Spirits who are dark master teachers and some factions of manipulating extraterrestrials, all serving themselves...

Most communication with any of these Spirits is in our dream state, but not always. The darker spirits are often present when one is manifesting very negative energy or abusing some substance and they exacerbate negative feelings or behavior.

Higher Angels are liaisons between the Divine Creator (heaven) and humanity. Angels can appear in any form that you are comfortable with. Stories about them come from all cultural/religious backgrounds. There are many different types, each specializing in various aspects of life and death experience. Some are personal angels who assist you throughout your life's journey. Others specialize in specific fields like play and happiness, business and finance, art and music, and health.

Certain beings are those who are specifically guardians for you, and others who are guardians for humanity and the planet as a whole. Angels were not created from any religious order on this planet, rather religious orders recognized their existence. Angels are from the heavenly realms of Light, members of our divine family heritage and they are here to be of service. As you welcome them in grattitude you will bring Divine Love/Light into your life.

Ascended human Spirit Guides usually have a specific goal and work with specific individuals and/or groups. Often, these guides were people we knew in past incarnations, who completed their earthly journeys and have already moved to a higher vibration of Light.

Some guides serve more than one person, such as ancestral guides, who would serve a family, clan or tribe. There are "group guides" who serve a private or commercial association or enterprise. The more expanded your consciousness, the more guides there are to assist you. Those of you who belong to groups have group guides as well. It doesn't matter whether you can see them or not, you can communicate with them when you are awake. Ask for open, clear communication. Specifically request guides who come in Divine Love Light, who are here to serve your highest purpose.

There are those of other realms who may come to you and say they are your Spirit Guides, for the purpose of manipulation. These can be the self-serving astral beings (discarnates). It is important to discern the difference between benevolent Higher Guidance and manipulative intruders. A simple question to ask is: "Are you in harmony with Divine Christ (or Buddhic) vibration, or higher?" If there is hesitation or any answer except "Yes," they are not.

Choose a specific time for daily communication with your guides. Request their assistance regarding your concerns. Honor them with respect in all of your inquiries. Practice speaking to them, simply and clearly; then be silent and practice Listening. The replies can come very quickly. You may think that it seems too easy—it is. Stay relaxed and allow the communication to flow. Trust the information that comes.

Include your inner child and your higher self in your communication sessions. Acknowledge and thank them for their assistance. Make offerings of flowers or other items. You can soon be communicating with them on a need to know basis, anywhere, anytime. Our attitude is the key—discernment is the tool—Divine Spirit is our guide. What a wonderful service! It is truly a blessing—treat it like one.

A New Cycle—An Awakening

There are many varied opinions regarding the New Age we are in, but all agree that something is happening. There are different opinions about exactly which Age it is, the most popular being The Aquarian Age, taken from one type of astrological viewpoint. Some refer to the ages as cycles. All the experts, past or present, agree that there will be great change as we pass from one cycle to the next, and that it would be wise to prepare ourselves. Many have lists on how we need to prepare, few agree on the amount of time we have to prepare. The estimates range from today, to fifty years hence. Perhaps we should begin now.

In reality, ALL life is cyclic. These cycles are a natural part of our evolutionary process. Most primitive cultures have names for these cycles and have prophecies regarding their effect on Earth and her inhabitants. Most religious or mystical prophecies describe similar scenarios. The stories are flavored by the different cultural influences, but the main threads of the prophecies are the same: the final phase manifests as world-wide chaos and cataclysmic destruction. Another cycle begins with renewal.

So, what do you think and feel about that? It's all very scary, if it is really happening in that way.

Expanded Awareness

Currently, there is much information from the philosophical, scientific and spiritual communities addressing the New Millenium, including changes in the plant, animal, and human inhabitants of this planet. Many scientists speak of the changes in tidal and weather patterns and an increase in earthquakes and volcanic eruptions. We can see for ouselves that these changes are upon us. There are those who say that a comet could collide with the earth or that solar flares will fry the surface of our planet. There are those who say we will destroy ourselves with nuclear war! There are others who said we were doomed by the "Y2k" issue.

It is my belief that we can minimize the effects of destructive THOUGHTS by eliminating our fearful reactions to the information. Whether it is channeled, prophesied or scientifically calculated, I believe that much of the information is filtered through an attitude of fear or intentionally created to "instill" fear. Fear weakens and disempowers those who embrace it.

I also believe that collective THOUGHT is the most powerful force in the Universe. What we need to do is direct our thoughts to our Highest Purpose! All the prophecies, predictions and calculations are dealing with a future possibility and probability or have been orchestrated for someone's hidden agenda. Another factor in future predictions is the fact that there are "parallel worlds." Which one are the prophets looking at? There is psychic/telepathic intrusion and mind implantation programming. Which prophets are being manipulated? Which ones are voices for those with a dark agenda for humanity? Are those concepts too horrible? Yes, you're damn right they are. Are they possible? Yes, unfortunately, they can be.

We must discern these prophecies—we can use them as gauges of how things could go—if we do not give attention to our responsibilities as Divine soul/spirits who are sustained by this living Planet-being, and each other.

Ultimately, natural changes serve the greater whole in the purpose of the renewal of our environment, the planet and humanity. Earth Changes are continuous and appear to be intensifying. There seems to be an increase of disruption on all levels of existence. We can tap into future events so that we can prepare for natural disruption. The way to flow with nature is to look and feel within the self. We all have this ability to expand our level of awareness. Our own body, mind and spirit will tell us what, where and when we need to know. But, we do need to be calm and still to hear it.

Our individual destiny is self-propelled on a soul level, but the details of our experiences, including the intensity of our reactions, are chosen by each of us as we move through our daily lives. Just as we have all chosen to be here at this time, I believe we can also choose to ease the effects of this transitional phase as we move into a new cycle. We can begin to do this by bringing Love and Joy into our hearts.

Personal Changes

This transitional process is simultaneously occurring inside ourselves physically, mentally, emotionally and spiritually. This is a natural part of our human evolutionary cycle. Most of us have experienced earth changes and shifts in human evolution in past incarnations but most of those memories are veiled. One of the changes that is taking place within us is an awakening process—the time to remember our past, a lifting of the veils. The state of amnesia has served an important purpose—allowing us focus in a given physical incarnation in order to concentrate on a current experience or lesson. This has been one of the aspects of the overall cycle that is coming to an end.

A metaphysical explanation of this cyclic re-birthing is that we are moving into a higher dimensional vibration. We are moving from third density to fourth and beyond. This is a faster vibrational frequency. Everything becomes lighter, literally: our planet, our bodies, our hearts, our lives. We are moving into a higher consciousness of love and harmony. All of our extra-senses are opening and being utilized naturally as our disharmonious attitudes are released. Our food requirements change and disease is decreased or eliminated as our emotional bodies are cleared and humanity evolves to a higher level of understanding and awareness, a higher quality of existence.

The changes taking place now stimulate a cleansing of the lower frequencies of negative thoughts, feelings and actions that have accumulated over thousands of years of earthly and other planetary incarnations. All that was not resolved, all that was not forgiven, is being presented now, individually and collectively. This is a final opportunity to balance all issues, all energies that are not in harmony.

The manifestation of these issues extensively permeate humankind: personal crisis can occur as negative karmic patterns are confronted, there is increased awareness of the need to improve physical and emotional health, hightened sensitivity to spiritual needs, stronger awareness and concern for the environment and it's non-human inhabitants, accelerated awareness and contact with non-physical energies and benevolent, helpful entities including angels and extraterrestrials, expanded awareness of life after death and personal exploration of altered states of consciousness, etc…

As our awareness expands, our desire is to move into harmony with nature and move away from our synthetic technology, which has become a detriment to our health on all levels. Many alternatives are being used in the fields of energy, healing, education and food production. New approaches are the "symptoms" of our awakening to the positive aspects needed to improve the quality of our lives and those of our children.

Planetary Changes

The earth has been and is being very affected by the disharmonious thoughts and actions of humanity. The planet Earth is a living being. The Earth's process of cleansing and balancing is manifesting in many ways: increasing earthquakes, volcanic eruptions, floods, droughts, other changes of atmospheric conditions, and changes of behavior in humans (as described above), animals, insects and micro-organisms—changes in the diseases, affecting all living things.

There is some resistance to the higher frequencies by those who prefer to hold on to negative patterns of fear, anger, greed and vengance. These negative patterns will be purged anyway, and will create greater discomfort and disruption to those who resist. Symptoms of resistance are many but all come from a base of intense fear or fear turned to anger.

An example of purging is the Middle East. It is the point on the planet where negative patterns have had the strongest reinforcement over the centuries. The original cause was, and still is, a belief in separation because of different-ness. This belief promotes feelings of superiority/inferiority, which create abuse of power.

All war is the outer manifestation of unresolved opposition within the self, that has been swallowed into the abysmal recesses of the human un-conscious, over many lifetimes, individually and collectively.

As a crisis counselor, I found that the Gulf war touched the deeper levels of feeling in everyone because it was televised for all to see on a daily basis. It triggered present and past-life traumas of being involved in War, internal and external, emotional and physical. Physical war is the outer manifestation of internalized negative feelings. War with another, always grows out of war with the self! The warring going on in the Slavic area of Europe is yet another example. War will continue as long as anyone feels superior or inferior to another, as long as one faction preys on another for their own gain.

Another event that had a global effect on everyone, was the death of Princess Diana. It was the very nature of her death, through violence, which stems from the word violate! It was a horrible, seemingly senseless loss of a persona who served and was loved by the masses. My heart was wrenched while watching the funeral on T.V. But I realized what a powerful catalyst it was to open the hearts of millions. Through grief and agony, there was an opportunity to release a great deal of accumulated pain, which can be a great healing. Eventually, we can all become aware of our immortality and realize that life continues, loved ones reunite and loss is only temporary.

Thought, when reinforced becomes feeling. Feeling, when reinforced, becomes action, positive or negative. As within, so without—we become what we believe. As negative feelings are repressed, they intensify. Eventually, they erupt, exaggerated, out of proportion, barely resembling the original negative thought from which it came, always born from a base of fear! Fear is the basis, the very root, the beginning of all negative thought and action. It is the one feeling we rarely express openly. We have been taught that it is weakness, a flaw, childish—an embarrassment, to be hidden, to be overcome—and certainly, never to be shown. "Don't let them know you are afraid—they will use it against you, take advantage of you, manipulate you"—(and "they" will and do).

Unexpressed, fear becomes repressed and altered into a defensive mode of anger. Anger repressed, becomes a war within the body, mind and spirit. It manifests physically as disease and war. War with family, then neighbors, then beyond. There is a growing excess of disease on our planet. Without healing—the continuation of war is inevitable!

Healing

We are all involved, directly or indirectly. A healing can take place. Without healing, wars will continue to strip the surface of the planet and the hearts of the people. We are all co-creators of humanity and we can all be co-creators of the healing of the heart of humanity.

We can begin "the healing" by bringing Love into our own hearts and Divine Light into our lives. We can heal the small battles within our selves by healing our relationships with each other. We can speak from our hearts to each others', always seeking the God within each person. Begin by reinforcing the love bonds with family and friends and setting our inner and outer houses in order.

Let go of all that is unused, unwanted or unworthy of our attention. Attend to all unfinished business both personal and professional, overdue debts and unexpressed feelings in a responsible way. Alter all words and actions that are not in harmony with Universal Principles. Begin now, to settle these issues. As these healings take place, a balance comes into our lives. We begin to like and respect the self and others. The key is to accept each other's differences and acknowledge the Divinity within us all. Ask for Higher Guidance in handling these matters. Go within your self and nurture your Inner Child—everyone has one. The Inner Child is the key to the higher Spirit Self, the Divine Being that we all truly are.

Know, that when we ignore our own Divinity by not following our Spirit, we create another dark space on this planet. As we share this healing energy with others, we are also healed. We are all channels for Divine Love/Light. We are the caretakers of this beautiful planet that sustains us, and we are the caretakers of each other!

We can share this Love/Light directly or send it from a distance, sharing it with all soldiers and civilians in war zones, personal and political. We can open our hearts and release the Love vibration out to them with the power of thought and the energy of feeling our intention. This does not compromise our desire for peace—it affirms it! War is profuse on our planet, individually and collectively. The time for blame is past—judgement does not heal anything—it creates separation. Angry protest against the symptoms (war), does not cure the cause (dis-ease), it feeds it!

Let us take responsibility for the privilege of Life itself and breathe happiness and prosperity into our world, which is being destroyed by the darkness of fear. There is no "God" outside of ourselves—who is going to step in and save us. The godly assistance we wait for exists within.

Awakening

Throughout these many cycles, the Earth has been a third-dimensional atmosphere of duality, or polarity. This polarity can be described as negative and positive, dark and light, contrary and harmonious. The limited density of physical matter is an illusion when we realize the true nature of our multidimensional reality. This we can do by expanding our consciousness and exploring the non-physical realms of our existence. We can percieve it as an aerial view. This can broaden and clarify our perspective. It is time for us all to re-evaluate our past and present paths, which will assist us in making healthy choices to enhance our future.

As we all experience the planetary changes, all of humanity is affected on every level of being. Those who are in resistance to the higher vibrations we are evolving into will become more contrary and violent, as their lower frequencies are aggitated. Others, who are in acceptance, will absorb and reflect more of the Light energy of Love, as their frequencies are accelerated. More fun, more joy, good health and prosperity—this is wonderful. We can access the heavenly realms and bring a bit of it into our earthly lives. This process has been described as coming into En-lighten-ment. It doesn't need a fancy name—it is simply, evolution. The evolution of ourselves, and the planet.

We have personal choices to make that will affect the whole of humanity as well as the self. It has been said that we can choose to move into higher consciousness now or return to a primeval third-dimensional existence and repeated cycles of re-incarnation and re-creation. Do we really know that? I feel there are many paths ahead of us. Wherever it is that we "go," we are immortal. Our spirit does not die. Our future is what we believe it will be. Whatever we fear or what we desire—whichever is stronger will be drawn to us…

There is no right or wrong choice. To become aware that "we" are truly responsible for all that happens to us IS our empowerment and our enlightenment—individually and collectively. If that feels like truth for you—then you've already got it!

Bibliography

Due to limited space, and a great number of books written on related subjects, I will only list a few of them here. I have chosen a wide variety, ranging from older classic works, to newsletters you can currently obtain through subscription. I encourage you to expand your research beyond this small list.

REFERENCE

Allison, Dr. Ralph: *Minds In Many Pieces*, 1980

Bletzer, June: *Donning International Encyclopedic Psychic Dictionary*, Donning Co. 1986, VA

De Angelis, Dr. Barbara: *How To Make Love All The Time*. Dell Books, 1991, NY

Egginton, Joyce: *From Cradle to Grave*, Jove Publications 1990, Berkley Publishing Group, NY

Fiore, Dr. Edith: *The Unquiet Dead*, Ballantine Books, 1987, New York, NY

Guiley, Rosemary Ellen: *Encyclopedia of Ghosts and Spirits*, Facts on File Inc., 1992, NY

Harper's Encyclopedia of Mystical & Paranormal Experience, Harper, 1991, San Francisco, CA

Gutmanis, June: *Na Pule Kahiko; Ancient Hawaiian Prayers*, Editions Limited, 1983, Honolulu, HI

Hoffman, Enid: *Huna, A Beginner's Guide*, Whitford Press, 1976, West Chester, PA.

Keyes, Daniel: *The Minds of Billy Milligan*, Bantam Books, 1982, NY

Norris, Joel: *Serial Killers*, Doubleday, 1988, New York, NY

Peck, M. Scott: *The People of The Lie*, Simon & Schuster, 1983, New York, NY

Phillips, Katherine A., M.D.: *The Broken Mirror*, Oxford University Press, 1996, NY

Pukui, M.K. & Elbert, S.: *Hawaiian Dictionary*, University of Hawaii Press 1986, Honolulu, HI

Sutphen, Dick: *50 Primary Universal Laws*, Audio Cassette, Valley of the Sun, Box 3004, Agoura Hills, CA

Thorndike & Barnhart: *World Book Dictionary*, Doubleday & Co. Inc.1982, New York, NY

Wickland, Dr. Carl A.: *Thirty Years Among The Dead*, Newcastle Publishing, 1974, Van Nuys, CA

SUGGESTED READING

Baldwin, Christina: *Calling the Circle*, Swan-Raven & Co., 1994, Newberg, OR

Bandler, Richard & Grindler, John: *Frogs Into Princes*, Real People Press, 1979 Moab, UT *The Structure of Magic I & II*, Science & Behavior Books, 1975, Palo Alto, CA

Brennan, Barbara Ann: *Hands of Light: A Guide to Healing Through the Human Energy Field*, Bantam Books, 1988, NY

Cousins, Norman: *Anatomy of an Illness*, Bantam Books, 1979, NY

Crabtree, Adam: *Multiple Man: Explorations in Possession and Multiple Personality*, Praeger, 1985, NY

Dalai Lama, His Holiness the Fourteenth: *Kindness, Clarity and Insight*, Snow LionPublications, 1984, NY

Ebon, Martin: *The Devil's Bride, Exorcism: Past & Present,* Harper & Row, 1974, NY

Feldman, Gail Carr, Ph.D.: *Lessons in Evil, Lessons From the Light,* Dell, 1993, NY

Fiore, Dr., Edith: *You Have Been Here Before,* Ballantine Books, 1978, NY

Fox, Matthew: *Original Blessing: A Primer in Creation Spirituality,* Bear & Co.,1983, Santa Fe, NM. *The Coming of the Cosmic Christ,* Harper & Row, 1988, San Francisco, CA

Francuch, Peter D.: *Principles of Spiritual Hypnosis,* Spiritual Advising Press, 1981Santa Barbara, CA

Gwain, Shakti: *Creative Visualization,* Whatever Publishing, 1978, Mill Valley, CA

Harner, Michael: *The Way of The Shaman,* Bantam Books, 1980, N.Y.

Hay, Louise L.: All Materials, Hay House Inc., P.O. BOX 2212, Santa Monica, CA

Ingerman, Sandra: *Mending the Fragmented Self,* Harper, 1991, S.F., CA

Ireland-Frey, Louise: *Clinical Depression: Releasement of Attached Entities from Unsuspecting Hosts, The Journal of Regression Therapy* 1, no.2 (Fall 86')

King, Serge: All Books, Quest Books, Wheaton, IL

Kubler-Ross, E.: All books, any publisher.

Laurence, Richard.: *The Book of Enoch the Prophet,* Wizards Bookshelf, 1977, San Diego, CA (original publication—1883, Kegan Paul, Trench & Co. London England)

Leadbeater, C.W.: *The Astral Plane,* Theosophical Publishing, 1984, Wheaton, IL, *The Chakras,* Theosophical Publishing, 1977, Wheaton, IL

Lee, Pali & Willis, Koko: *Tales from the Night Rainbow,* Pali, Kapela, Wills 'Ohana Inc. 1759 Iwi Way, Honolulu, HI 96816

Long, Max Freedom: All Books, any Publisher

Mack, Dr. John, PhD.: *Abducted*, Random House, 1995, NY

Moody, Raymond: *Life After Life*, Bantam Books, 1976, NY

Motoyama, Hiroshi, PhD.: *"Bodily Healing Through Releasement,"* The Journal of *Regression Therapy 2*, No. 2 (Fall 1987)

Platt, Rutherford H., Jr.: *The Forgotten Books of Eden*, Bell Publishing Co., 1980, NY

Pukui, M.K., Haertig, E.W., & Lee, C.A.: *Nana I Ke Kumu (Look to the Source)*,VOL. 1 & 2, Queen Liliuokalani Trust, 1972, Honolulu, Hi.

Rogo, D. Scott: *The Infinite Boundary*, Dodd & Mead & Co., 1987, New York, NY

Schwarz, Jack: *It's Not What You Eat But What Eats You*, Celestial Arts, 1988, Berkeley, CA

Siegel, Bernie: All books, any publisher

Sitchin, Zacharia: All Books, any Publisher

Steiger, Brad: All Books, any Publisher

Sutphen, Dick: All related books and cassettes, Valley of the Sun., CA

Swedenborg, Emmanuel: All Books, any Publisher

Valerian, Valdamar: *Matrix II, III & IV*, *The Leading Edge Newsletter*, Leading Edge Research, Yelm,WA

Von Daniken, Eric: All Books, any Publisher

Waters, Frank: *Book of the Hopi*, Ballantine Books, 1963, New York, NY

White, Ellen G.: *Cosmic Conflict*, Pacific Press, 1988, Boise, Id (original publication—1888 as *The Great Controversy*)

Whitton, Joel L. & Fisher, Joe: *Life Between Life*, Warner Books, 1986, New York

Woodrew, Greta: *On A Slide of Light*, Macmillan Publishing Co., 1981, New York

Zambucka, Kristin: *Ano Ano, The Seed*, Mana Publishing Co., 1984, Honolulu, HI *The Keepers of The Earth*, Harrane Publishing Co., 1985, Honolulu, HI

RELIGIOUS TITLES

The Apocrypha

The Pseudepigrapha

Catholic Encyclopedia

And any others you feel drawn to.

Index

193

0-595-31198-9

Printed in Great Britain
by Amazon